THE OSHU KENDO RENMEI

A History of British and European Kendo (1885-1974)

By Paul Budden

Bunkasha International — Chiba, Japan

Copyright © 2017 Paul Budden. All Rights Reserved.

ISBN 978-4-907009-23-6

*This edition is dedicated to Roald Knutsen
for his outstanding efforts in establishing the kendo we have today
in the U.K. and Europe.*

This book is also dedicated to the memory of Fujii Okimitsu-sensei who sadly passed away while this book was being prepared for publication. Fujii-sensei left an indelible mark on kendo in the U.K.

Personal Acknowledgements

I would like to thank Roald Knutsen, Fujii Okimitsu, Jacques Dupont, Ian Parker-Dodd, Kurata Yoshihiro, Takizawa Kenji, Ozawa Hiroshi, Per Ybo, George McCall, Chris Buxton, Clive Sinclaire and The To-Ken Society, Michel Bouscary, John Bowen, Alain Floquet and Jean-Marc Papadacci. A special thanks to Professor Nagao Susumu for his extensive research in Japan. He is a professor at the School of Global Japanese Studies at Meiji University in Tokyo, Japan. His research themes include characteristics of budo and issues associated with its internationalisation. He is also kendo Kyoshi 8-dan. To Sir Hugh Cortazzi for his support and guidance.

Also, a special thanks to Matsuda Kazuyo for her translation work undertaken for this book. She is dojo leader at the Kodokan Kendo Club in Watford, England, and holds the grade of Renshi 7-dan in kendo, and works as an architect and translator.

Chris Buxton is a British Kendo Association iaido Kyōshi 7-dan and jodo Kyōshi 7-dan at the Eishinkan Dojo.

I would also like to express my gratitude to Alex Bennett, Michael Ishimatsu-Prime, Bryan Peterson, Baptiste Tavernier, and Trevor Jones of Kendo World for their editorial guidance.

Contents

INTRODUCTION	9
CHAPTER 1: The First Age of British Kendo	15
CHAPTER 2: Kendo Emerges from the Shadows	21
CHAPTER 3: Humble Beginning and Japanese Connections	25
CHAPTER 4: Genesis of the European Kendo Renmei	35
CHAPTER 5: The Bumpy Road from Renmei to Federation	43
CHAPTER 6: Across the Channel Kendo in France	51
CHAPTER 7: A Parting of the 'Ways'	59
CHAPTER 8: The Inaugural European Kendo Tournaments	63
CONCLUSION	77
APPENDIX 1: Fujii Okimitsu	81
APPENDIX 2: Roald Knutsen	87

Introduction

The first display of Japanese swordsmanship in the UK can be attributed to a demonstration at Tannaker Buhicrosan's Japanese Village in Knightsbridge, London, in 1885. (See Chapter 1) In Tokyo in 2015, I met with Japanese author, Kurata Yoshihiro, to discuss his 1983 book on the Japanese Village.[1] Using original records, we were able to find the names of the four kenshi involved: Tominaga Moritoshi (40), Baba Shin'ichi (33), Hidaka Takeshi (45) and Nozaki Yoshide (50). Tominaga and Baba were both residing in Kanagawa. Hidaka was born and living in Nagasaki; Nozaki was born in Ehime and also living in Nagasaki. Both Hidaka and Nozaki, who were described as "warrior class", embarked from Nagasaki.

Further research by Professor Nagao Susumu found Tominaga in the banzuke (ranking list) of the Yokohama gekken-kai (public shows of swordsmanship) held at Matsugae-chō (modern-day Naka ward) in Yokohama. In April 1884, he was ranked maegashira, a high rank which is more commonly associated with sumo, but was also used in the registration of gekken fighters at that time.

According to their schedule, the four kenshi would have demonstrated *kenjutsu* together twice daily with added performances on Sundays for the two years of the Japanese Village's existence. The duration of the displays is believed to have been around 45 minutes per session.[2]

The rather 'tongue in cheek' consensus is that, at the very least, they must have become very close friends, and surely revelled in their time spent in England. It appears that Hidaka enjoyed it so much that he was ordered to return to Japan in March 1885 (just after the village had opened) because of his excessive drinking habits, something he had probably acquired in his native land. No further records of the four kenshi have been found after 1887, when they would have returned following the closure of the Japanese Village.

明治17年4月，横浜撃剣会 横浜松ヶ枝町（石垣氏蔵）

The banzuke (ranking list) of the Yokohama gekken-kai[3]

---

1 Kurata Yoshiro. *1885 Japan in London*. Tokyo: Mainichi Shinbunsha, February 20, 1983.

2 Ibid., p.74

3 Ishigaki Yasuzo-sensei, (former head of the Jikishin Kage-ryū school) *banzuke* from *Shiryō Meiji Budō-shi*, Ichirō Watanabe (ed.), p. 734.

Fencers at the Japanese Village 1885 [5]

Professor Nagao mentions that he could not find any of the names of these four in the directory of swordsmen in Meiji and Taisho periods. They were possibly skilful swordsmen, but were certainly not famous. Their reason for going to England was perhaps due to the extremely hard living conditions that former warriors and martial artists were experiencing in Japan in those early years of modernisation.

There were less than flattering views surrounding the integrity of the Japanese village. It was considered a "low-class" venture, and not truly representative of how the new, modern Japan wished to be seen at the time.[4] Professor Nagao expressed caution in evaluating the actual skill level of the four swordsmen involved, having some reservations after examining this background information.

It would take some 72 years after these inaugural displays at the Japanese Village for kendo to come into its own in England. When kendo was first practised in the UK rather than just being demonstrated in the early part of the twentieth century, it had been very much under the control of judo clubs. Namely, the Budokwai and Anglo Japanese Jujutsu and Martial Arts Association (later known as the Anglo Japanese Judo Club). The discovery by Roald Knutsen of three sets of kendo armour at the London Judo Society (LJS; an offshoot of the Budokwai) in Vauxhall, in October 1957, would at last serve to establish kendo in its own right when he began to study it in earnest the following year. R.A. Lidstone then joined him in 1959 at the London Judo Society, the home of the Shinto Ryu Kendo Club from 1957.

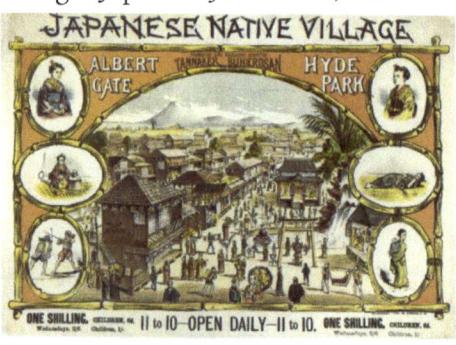

Japanese Village Poster [6]

During our numerous discussions, Roald Knutsen (now in his 80s) talked of the rather ambitious days in the early 1960s when he and his wife Patricia, R.A. Lidstone, and Sweden-based Hungarian

---

4 Kurata Yoshiro, 11, 24–28.

5 The Japanese Village Posters were produced by Theophilus Creber, who were popular circus and show poster printers based in Plymouth, England. 1878–1889. The British Library "Posters of the Japanese Village".

6 Ibid.

Count Robert von Sandor[7], who was studying, practising, and teaching various Japanese martial arts, wanted to get kendo and iaido established in Europe. This would be achieved by co-ordinating several national groups in other countries that were beginning to express interest as kendo started to burgeon in the UK.

Knutsen elaborated:

> "Our first group formed from mainly judo friends at the London Judo Society, following my suggestion to George Chew (6-dan judo sensei) about using the armour. There was no kendo, of course, only the three kendo *bōgu* and some *shinai* all donated by the Japanese Honorary Chairman of the London Judo Society, Hatta Ichirō-sensei.[8] Chew-sensei readily agreed, but with a stipulation that I also continued judo. I followed his directive for a while, but kendo soon took preference. Chew-sensei did not oppose this development, offering only support and encouragement."

Kanō Jigorō with Hatta Ichirō in 1937

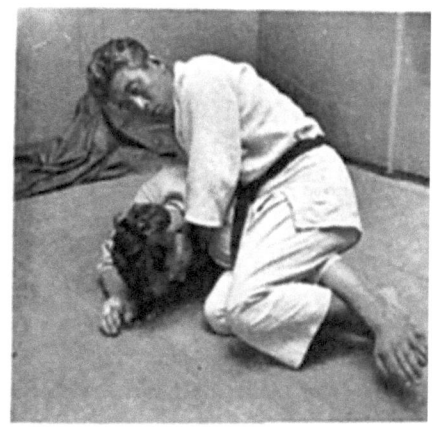

Hatta in England – Date unknown

After observing kendo training sessions at the Shinto Ryu Club within the LJS, Hatta Ichirō realised that they were serious students and worth encouraging. He made an initial introduction a year or so later to the relatively newly formed organisation responsible for kendo in Japan, the Zen Nihon Kendo Renmei (All Japan Kendo Federation).

Another Japanese martial artist, Yamada Senta, became the chief judo instructor of the LJS club in 1959. He was acquainted with Takizawa Kōzō Hanshi and Hatta. Both Yamada and Hatta were aikido students, and instructors under Tomiki Kenji.

---

7 For a list of Count Robert von Sandor's achievements and interests, see the following profile: http://prabook.org/web/person-view.html?profileId=86091 Accessed October 2015.

8 For more information on Hatta Ichiro, see Budden, Paul. *A Truly British Samurai*. Chiba: Bunka-sha International, 2015, p 49.

Hatta had already visited London in 1935 when he accompanied an English woman, Sarah Mayer, the first foreign female to be awarded *shodan* (1-dan) in judo in Japan. At that time, he also met with Charles Boxer at the London Budokwai. As an aside, I had an interesting conversation with Ozawa Hiroshi-sensei about Hatta. He recalled practising with him as a young man when he went to the Noma Dojo in Tokyo with his father, Ozawa Takashi, and the famous novelist Mishima Yukio. Roald Knutsen mentioned Hatta's contribution to promoting the martial arts in England:

> "Because of Hatta-sensei's long association with budo here from before the war, and knowing Charles Boxer from that time, he was clearly active in supporting the LJS. I believe this was an off-shoot of the Budokwai, although I was unaware of this in my judo days. I recall Lidstone-sensei telling me of him also having met Boxer before the Second World War."

This corroborates my assertion in *A Truly British Samurai* that Boxer may have been aware of R.A. Lidstone.[9] Knutsen is quite certain that the initial contacts with His Excellency Yukawa Morio at the Embassy of Japan, and then with the AJKF also came through the good offices of Hatta Ichirō. These connections were essential to the growth of kendo in the UK. Furthermore, Takizawa Kenji recounted that the armour Knutsen discovered had been carried by members of Hatta's wrestling teams when they visited the UK.

> "The three kendo *bōgu* presented by Hatta-sensei to the LJS in the early 1950s were of good quality; bamboo *dō* in brown leather, not black lacquer. The Eikoku Kendo Renmei purchased them later on, and they are still in use."

Little did he know at the time that his discovery of the *bōgu* and his subsequent interest in kendo would be an historical event that, in many ways, contributed greatly to the development of kendo throughout Europe. Patricia Knutsen, wife of Roald, although perhaps known better for her naginata training, is in fact believed to be the first British female to study and practise kendo. It is possible that their son Alexander and his sister Lynne were then the first junior members in the country to take up both kendo and iaido, like their father. This justifies the statement by Knutsen in a letter to Takizawa Kōzō on July 5, 1968: "We are truly a budo family at last." This little volume will hopefully bring light to Knutsen's small but significant discovery, and how this led to the growth of the greater European kendo family.

---

9 Ibid. p 52.

CHAPTER 1

The First Age of British Kendo

Japanese Ways of Chivalry drawn by Samuel Begg for the Illustrated London News, 1919

The Royal Armouries possess sets of samurai armour that were sent as gifts by Tokugawa Hidetada to King James I, via John Saris in 1613. However, the first public reference to Japanese kendo armour was in a *Liverpool Mercury* newspaper advertisement dated December 12, 1865:

> WITHOUT RESERVE
> On Thursday next, the 14th instant, at Two o'clock, at the
> Brokers Office. Colonial-buildings 36, Dale-street,
> 200 Open Japanese FANS,
> A Quality IVORY CURIOSITIES,
> A Suit of Japanese FENCING ARMOUR,
> A Quality LEATHER, PAPER, Ac, Ac.
> For further particulars apply to
> MALCOM GREAME & C0., 36, Dale-street.

In 1862 the Japanese sent their first official representatives to Europe, since first contact was made in the sixteenth and seventeenth centuries. At the World Fair in Paris in 1867, the arts and artifacts in the Japanese exhibition aroused great interest.

Fascination in things Japanese continued to rise culminating in 1885 with the opening of the Japanese village in Knightsbridge London.[1]

At Tannaker Buhicrosan's Japanese Village in Knightsbridge, according to pictorial records and newspaper articles of the time, there were daily demonstrations of kendo often described as 'Fencing and Single Stick Exercise' and sumo.

> Yesterday a numerous party were invited to a private inspection, and after lunch were entertained with an exhibition of Japanese fencing, wrestling, and dancing in the theatre attached to the Village. The fencing with bamboo canes, between two athletes, padded and wearing wire masks, caused considerable amusement and the performers certainly displayed considerable adroitness. The wrestling was rather slow and, according to English notions of the exercise, *extremely Tame*.[2]

It seems that there had been displays of kendo equipment at the International Health exhibition of 1884 as according to a January 12, 1885, extract from *The Times* found in the British Kendo Association History: "The fencing, as those who saw the display of masks, pads, gloves and bamboo swords sent from Tokyo gymnasium to the Health Exhibition".[3]

According to a newspaper article dated May 23, 1898, the crew of the Japanese imperial navy cruiser Takasago entertained an audience in Tyneside with entertainment that included kendo.[4] British newspaper archives of the time report further displays of kendo performed by crews of visiting Japanese ships. Many of Japan's first naval vessels were built in British yards and a close relationship developed between the Royal Navy and the Japanese navy both before and following the first Anglo-Japanese Alliance of 1902.

In Victorian Britain fencing had fallen into decline. Killing someone in a duel was seen as murder; in 1844 an act of Parliament denied army widows a pension if their husband died as the result of a duel. It was only through the efforts of such people as Alfred Hutton and Egerton Castle that serious knowledge of British swordsmanship was retained. Japan was in a similar situation in that the long tradition of the sword was being lost. The popularity of kendo had declined in Japan after the Meiji Restoration in 1868 and the abolition of the right of samurai to carry swords in 1876. The tradition was probably saved partly by Sakakibara Kenichi, who had formed a fencing company of redundant samurai and from 1873 had given exhibitions of swordsmanship and martial arts to the general public.

---

1 For a description of the village and information about Tannaker Buhicrosan see Cortazzi, Hugh. *Japan in Late Victorian London: The Japanese Village in Knightsbridge and the Mikado, 1885*, Sainsbury Institute for the Study of Japanese Arts and Cultures (SISJAC), Norwich, 2009

2 The *London Standard*, January 10, 1885

3 Howell, John. "History of the BKA", The British Kendo Association, 2005. http://www.british-kendoassociation.com/history-of-the-bka/

4 *The Newcastle Daily Chronicle*, May 24, 1898.

Kendo and fencing could no longer be regarded as utilitarian activities, so they had to become sport, entertainment or education. Kendo was seen as contributing to the development of character and so used sporting type competition in order to assist the process.

Prior to the formation in 1895 of the Dai-Nippon Butokukai as the main governing body for the martial arts in Japan, Japanese swordsmanship was traditionally referred to as *kenjutsu* and the sporting form as *gekken*. The term kendo was adopted in 1920. Similarly, judo, another of the Japanese martial arts, had been called *jujutsu* or *jujitsu*.

Francis James Norman, a former British cavalryman, who taught at the Naval Academy in Etajima from 1888, studied *jujutsu* and *kenjutsu* as well as sumo and Japanese military history. After his return to London in November 1905 he gave demonstrations of *jujutsu* and *kenjutsu* at the Marlborough Hall Polytechnic in Regent Street. Instructors present included Kanaya, Tani, Miyake, Fujisake, Eida, Miss Roberts, F.J. Norman, Sergeant-Major Betts, and some pupils from the Japanese School of Ju-jitsu, 305 Oxford Street. *Jujutsu* and *kenjutsu* were expounded in Norman's short book *The Fighting Man of Japan: The training and exercises of the Samurai*.[5] This book records the time when kendo and judo were still in their formative stages.

Koizumi Gunji[6] arrived in Wales in 1906. He was to play an important role in Britain in the promotion of judo and kendo, which he had begun at the age of twelve.

On his arrival in England in 1909 Mishiku Kaoru quickly took over the running of the Anglo Japanese Jujutsu and Martial Arts Association at its new venue in Strathmore Gardens, London. Mishiku, who was a graduate of the Sekai Butokukai (the premier martial arts university of Japan) and a master of judo, *jujutsu* and kendo, employed various Japanese teachers at the club.

In 1918 Koizumi started the Budokwai Judo Club in London. He thought that the promotion of *jujutsu* and *kenjutsu* might help his adopted country writing::

> I hope that rendering my service in promoting such training would be a means of pacifying my conscience, which was pricked by the fact that we Japanese, especially students, had been the recipients of the kindness, hospitality and generously bestowed by the people of this country, without making any tangible return.[7]

Kendo demonstrations were held at cultural evenings as well as at training sessions. At these evenings in addition to kendo demonstrations lectures were given on Japanese

---

5 Norman, F.J. *The Fighting Man of Japan: the training and exercises of the Samurai*. Bunkasha International, Chiba: 2013.

6 See biographical portrait by Richard Bowen in Hugh Cortazzi, Hugh ed. *Britain and Japan: Biographical Portraits*, Volume IV, Japan Library, London 2002. p.312.

7 Bowen, Richard. "Its Roots and Early History and Some Other Early Matters", The Budokwai, 1999. http://www.budokwai.net/history_vol_i.htm See also the personal writings Richard Bowen, British Judo pioneer, who was a 4-dan and Vice-president of the Budokwai, e.g. *100 Years of Judo in Great Britain*. There are further notes not included in the book, which are on file in the Richard Bowen Archive in Bath University.

poetry, Buddhism, history, wood block prints and exhibitions were held of paintings by resident Japanese artists such as Yoshio Markino.

Because of the strange noises and crashes that came from the building, it became the custom to invite the neighbours to these lectures and other events to show how odd but harmless the members were. Many years later *The Budokwai Bulletin* describing the early days of the society recorded an occasion when, '... anxious neighbours, horrified by the thuds and shrieks and fearing someone was being tortured, hastily summoned the police.' One lecture was devoted to the art of the *kiai* used in kendo.

The first Budokwai display was held at the club in Lower Grosvenor Place, Victoria in 1918. The second Budokwai demonstration took place at the Aeolian Hall in London in 1919 and it became an annual event.

Visiting kendo master Sonobe Masatada gave the opening address at Aeolian Hall in London on May 31, 1919, and demonstrated aspects of kendo, *nabebuta* (the use of saucepan lids in self-defence), *kusarigama* (chain and sickle) and *nitō* (the use of two swords). Sonobe was the husband of Sonobe Hideo a famous naginata (halberd) teacher. The naginata display at the Aeolean, however, was demonstrated by a Mme Hino Yoshiko who was in London with her husband, who also took part in the kendo display.

According to Budokwai records a number of kendo displays by members of the Anglo Japanese Jujutsu and Martial Arts Association took place in 1923. In the following year the famous Japanese film star Hayakawa Sessue**,** best known in Britain for his performance in *Bridge over the River Kwai*, gave a display of kendo at the Budokwai's annual demonstration at the Stadium Club in High Holborn.

In the following years up to the beginning of the Second World War the Budokwai and the Anglo Japanese Jujutsu and Martial Arts Association, which was renamed the Anglo Japanese Judo Club by Mishiku in 1929, continued to promote judo and also teach kendo. Its kendo instructor from 1931 was Okamoto Yoshitomo.

R.A. Lidstone, who had first seen a demonstration of kendo in New Zealand by Japanese sailors, began to study kendo in late 1930 or early 1931. He made steady progress and was promoted to 6-kyu in 1936. In 1937 he was selected to take part in a kendo demonstration for Prince Chichibu at a garden party in his honour at the Hurlingham Sport Club, in Fulham London.

Kendo demonstrations were filmed by Pathe News in 1936. Okamoto Yoshitomo and Kudzutani Arataro demonstrated Japanese sword techniques at the Holborn Stadium. The following year demonstrations of Japanese sword techniques were given at the Anglo Japanese Judo Club by Mishiku and Okamoto.

The war years for the most part brought an end to the practice of Japanese martial arts at the clubs. Following the war, Mishiku, who died in 1972, worked hard to rebuild the Anglo Japanese Judo Club, which moved to Sandycombe Road in Kew. The Budokwai also reconvened moving to its current location in South Kensington in 1954.

CHAPTER 2

Kendo Emerges from the Shadows

The following picture is not of British Kendo Association or British Kendo Council members, but is of judoka from the Budokwai in 1958.¹ It shows an interesting way of tying the *men-himo* across the front of *mengane* and at the back. Or, maybe it had just come undone.

We know that the Budokwai and other judo dojo had been instrumental in the introduction of kendo in the UK through Koizumi Gunji, Mishiku Kaoru and other judo pioneers in the early part of the twentieth century. The 1919 demonstration at the Aeolian Halls, the demonstration for Prince Chichibu in Hurlingham in 1936, and Pathe News film clips from the same period are proof of this. However, this photo is the first pictorial confirmation that kendo had at least periodically restarted in the judo clubs following the end of the Second World War.

As a part of the ongoing development of kendo in the UK, Roald Knutsen, together with his wife Patricia and R.A. Lidstone, set up a rival organisation to the British Kendo Council, the British Kendo Association

Pictures 7 & 8: Judo magazine 1958 with small caption picture underneath

(BKA) in 1962. Before this period there were no official organisations for kendo; it was randomly practised at judo clubs in the UK, but mainly around London.² They received support from kendo notaries including Dr. Benjamin H. Hazard from the United States. Ōya Kazuo Hanshi, Chief Director of the AJKF, was also supportive of the development of kendo outside Japan, and many other high-ranking Japanese kendoka were enthusiastic to help under his guidance. According to Knutsen,

"By this time we were greatly supported by the then Japanese Ambassador in

---

1 *Judo Magazine* Vol.3. No.3. Croyden, Surrey: Judo Limited, December 1958, Front cover.
2 Budden, Paul. *A Man of Many Parts. Part 2: The Old Vic, Robin Hood and Rashomon.* in Kendo World Vol. 7.3. Chiba, Bunkasha International. December 2014.

> London, His Excellency Yukawa Morio, himself a pre-WWII kendo 4-dan. The AJKF arranged a visit from Takizawa Kōzō-sensei, then Kyōshi 7-dan. After this first direct contact, Lidstone-sensei, Patricia and myself decided it was time to form the Eikoku Kendo Renmei. The original British Kendo Association or BKA as it became known, was constituted in 1962. I have always preferred to use the Japanese terminology, Eikoku Kendo Renmei, because that title was better understood in Japan."

Shortly after Lidstone joined them at the Shinto Ryu, they received a gift from Japan—a small kendo book from Yuno Masanori Hanshi in Tokyo. It later transpired that this gift was thanks to an introduction from Hatta. Yuno would remain a staunch supporter of the BKA until he passed away in the early 1980s.

According to Professor Nagao Susumu, Yuno graduated from Tokyo Higher Normal School (now the University of Tsukuba), so he is in effect his *senpai*[3] (Professor Nagao is also a graduate of the same university). Yuno's teachers were a veritable who's who of kendo legends: Takano Sasaburō, Sugawara Tōru, Satō Ukichi, Morita Bunjūrō, and Mitsuhashi Hidezō. Later, he also studied with the preeminent Ogawa Chūtarō-sensei.

Knutsen pointed out that despite kendo being tiny in comparison to judo, and later to karate and aikido, they were right in the centre of budo's gradual boom in Europe, and the small kendo fraternity benefitted from many well-informed contacts and advisors.

> "Lidstone-sensei was a godsend, of course, and even more so was the close advisory contact with Benjamin H. Hazard-sensei. In a lesser, more figurehead role was Sir Frank Bowden, Bt., but, apart from trying to mend fences, he didn't interfere in kendo matters despite being a most generous supporter."

Knutsen only actually met Hazard in person for the first time at the Tokyo Saineikan Dojo at the Imperial Palace in 1967, some ten years after they began to correspond. The enthusiasm of the Knutsens, Lidstone, and Hazard together with the first few new recruits at the Shinto Ryu dojo would provide the impetus to develop and cultivate the initial contacts made by Hatta-sensei which would lead to actual physical support from individuals in Japan and the newly formed AJKF.

---

[3] The Japanese word *"senpai"* refers to someone of a higher age or one's senior, whereas *"kōhai"* is one's junior.

CHAPTER 3

Humble Beginning and Japanese Connections

As a result of support from Japan, visits to the UK by high ranking teachers happened from as early as June 1962. Distinguished sensei were often seen teaching and practising at the various dojo around the country, including the Shinto Ryu dojo in London. Nakamura Kishirō (7-dan) was the very first senior instructor to visit in this new period of British kendo. He was accompanied by Takizawa Kōzō. Both were council members of the AJKF which later awarded the title of Renshi to Roald Knutsen on the strength of that visit, and for his considerable efforts in promoting kendo in the region. This was a great achievement as he only held the rank of 3-dan at the time. Ōura Yoshihiko (7-dan) and Takami Taizō, a 4-dan and a sculptor, visited the UK during 1963. The first Hanshi 9-dan to visit was Koshikawa Hidenosuke of the Osaka Kendo Federation in November 1964.

Hanshi 9-dan Koshikawa Hidenosuke, and with Roald Knutsen, circa 1964

In August 1966, Arai Shigeo (later 8-dan), a high-level *nitō* player and respected businessman from Osaka, came to England after sending a letter of introduction. In an early report for the British Kendo Association, Knutsen chronicled conversations with Arai Shigeo (Kyōshi 7-dan) who visited the Butokukan Kendo Dojo in Brighton.[1] Knutsen wrote:

> "Mr Arai traced his family line through sixteen generations of samurai who were

---

1 Knutsen, Roald. "Report for the British Kendo Association", August 4, 1966, pp. 2–3.

middle-ranking retainers of the Yonezawa clan in northeast Japan. His grandfather had been an engineer for the Yonezawas before the Meiji Restoration while his grandmother had given instruction in the use of the *kusarigama* (the chain and sickle). After the Restoration, Mr. Arai's parents had felt that all the military equipment owned by the family—spears, bows, swords, etc.—would no longer be of any use, and sold everything around the middle of the Meiji period."[2]

Arai was a graduate of the Tokyo University of Foreign Studies, and was the captain of his university kendo team. Before the Second World War, he had spent 15 years in Western Malaya as the manager of an iron mine, and had taught kendo there to the many Japanese employees. A nephew of Sir Winston Churchill, who later became the High Commissioner of Northern Malaya, had been very interested in kendo and actually received instruction from Arai.

During the Japanese military occupation of Malaya, Arai continued to practise kendo with the resident army officers who lived in the neighbourhood of the mine. At the end of the hostilities, he was interned at Singapore and repatriated to Japan after three months of captivity.

The author Nevil Shute (second from the left) in front of Item Willie (a plane) at Khota Bahru in Malaya on February 17, 1949. On Shute's left is Mr Churchill, the area's British Adviser and a nephew of Winston Churchill

After the Second World War Arai became the manager of a well-known Anglo-Japanese shipping agent in Osaka and Kobe—Butterfield and Swire Ltd. When it was learned that he would be visiting England, he was asked by Hanshi 9-dan

---

2 Ibid.

Nenriki Dojo circa 1969. Holt-sensei nearest to the camera

Bushi Budokai Portsmouth 1964

Koshikawa Hidenosuke and other members of the International Businessmen's Kendo Renmei in Osaka to meet with the British Kendo Association and prepare the ground for closer relations.

A young woman by the name of Horie Etsuko (2-dan) came to the UK for about one year in 1964.[3] Being a graduate of Hosei University she was a junior of Fujii Okimitsu. Horie also met with Benjamin Hazard in Japan, who then introduced her to Roald Knutsen. Knutsen in turn invited her to visit England. When it was decided that she would visit the UK, particular attention was given to improving her technical ability. She wondered what she could do to help as she felt her understanding of kendo was quite limited. She was actively encouraged by the instructor at Hosei University, Maruyama Giichi, and Takizawa Kōzō and Watanabe Toshio of the AJKF. Horie arrived in England on November 5, 1964, travelling alone with *shinai* and a suitcase. The *shinai* caused some concern with British customs, and she had to give a lengthy explanation of what it was used for in order to be allowed to bring it into the country.[4]

Horie began training at the Shinto Ryu club in London, and was quite embarrassed to be greeted and treated as a teacher on her first visit. There were serious collectors of swords, armour, and Japanese paraphernalia practising at the time, and her visits always attracted questions on all matters pertaining to kendo, requiring her to research further to offer suitable explanations. She once commented that they "didn't know very much", and were wearing *keiko-gi* over *hakama*; most of their knowledge was coming from a limited supply of books available on kendo and Japanese history in public libraries, and also films. One can easily imagine some of the

---
3 Koshikawa Shunosuke, *Budō Hyōron 6th Magazine No.2*. Budō Hyōronsha, Tokyo: 1965, p.34-35.
4 Etsuko Horie, "Kendo Journey to Europe". In *Budo Hyōron 6th Magazine No.2* Budo Hyōronsha, Tokyo: 1965, p36-38.

At Hosei University dojo, Tokyo. Maruyama Giichi (7-dan) instructing Horie Etsuko (2-dan) watched by Sakamoto Micko (3-dan). Circa 1963

styles of kendo being displayed, with notions of *Seven Samurai* and duels under the cherry blossoms at dawn. In spite of the somewhat surreal world she found herself in, she gave them every respect for their sincere efforts, and they studied hard.

Horie often referred to Knutsen as the "English Musashi" and to Benjamin Hazard, who supported and helped Knutsen throughout these formative years, as the "American Musashi". Coincidently Musashi was the pen name that Knutsen used for the kendo related articles and reports in the *Judo Magazine*.

Kendo in Europe, unlike judo, struggled to retain members. Opportunities to train, grade, and compete were few and far between, so when promotion examinations were held in London twice a year, people from all over the country would attend. Horie noted that there was a second group of kendo practitioners active in various places around the UK. The young man in charge was a Japanese 2-dan who was tireless in his efforts to promote the art, and travelled great distances to do so. I believe that this was most likely Otani Tomio, as Horie mentions that he would often be accompanied by other visiting budo sensei from the IBC (International Budo Council, Abe Kenshirō's organisation).[5] The main problems from her perspective was the lack of an experienced Japanese teacher who could teach correct kendo. (This was before Fujii-sensei arrived.) Also, kendo equipment was both expensive and difficult to obtain. Horie urged the AJKF to help more to rectify these problems.

Otani ran three clubs in London and provided information on kendo through articles in various journals, one of which appeared in *The Japanese Fighting Arts*.[6] This article, written when kendo in Britain was still floundering in its infancy, demonstrates the depth of his understanding of kendo and includes clear explanations of both the technical terms and kendo philosophy.

---

5 Kenshiro Abe (December 15, 1915–December 1, 1985) was a prominent Japanese master of judo, aikido, and kendo. He had introduced aikido to the United Kingdom in 1955.

6 *The Japanese Fighting Arts* 1967. Letchworth, Herts: Garden City Press Ltd.

Specialising in kendo, iaido and aikido in 1961 Otani was graded *shodan* and appointed the National Coach for kendo by Abe-sensei (The British Kendo Council). A year later he received 2-dan in "budo", which was a general award for the martial arts including kendo covered by Abe's IBC organisation. Sources say he was awarded 5-dan in budo before Abe-sensei left for Japan, but Otani-sensei never spoke of the grades he had acquired.

The first 'kendo only' club in Britain opened in 1961 the Acton Kendo Kyushinkan, formed under the auspices of the British Kendo Council, an offshoot of Abe's IBC and run by Otani-sensei.

Horie was probably the first Japanese female kendoka to visit and reside in the UK, and she helped through translation, explanation, and by actively instructing the beginners and lower grades. Being an extremely humble individual, she would invariably insist she was only a student. After returning to Japan, Horie later moved to Sweden where she attended university. She qualified as a teacher and worked at an elementary school in Malmo. She was instrumental in starting kendo in Malmo, and was key in Sweden's kendo development. Horie married Japanese art specialist Kjell Lindberg after first meeting in 1965. She remained active in Swedish kendo until her death in 2005. The Etsuko Cup is held annually in her memory.

Horie Etsuko Standing. Back row second from the right Summer Training in Japan, August 1963

Another Japanese individual who Knutsen took under his wing was Ōsaki Shintarō, a student of Dr. Itō Kyoitsu of Tokyo. According to Knutsen, Ōsaki was a great help in those early years, and he had apparently been commanded by Itō to ensure that Knutsen learnt the Nihon Kendo Kata correctly.

"We spent four days in Battersea one long weekend guarding an empty warehouse premises for a friend of mine just practising the *kata* six hours or more each day. I have never forgotten this experience." (Knutsen)

Ōsaki was originally from Toyama prefecture, and had only passed the grade of *shodan*. According to Knutsen, however, this was because "he refused to take any other formal rank on principle". He lived at the Knutsen's house for over a year while studying cooking technology at the Borough Polytechnic (now the South

The trophy of the Etsuko Cup. It is a small vase that Etsuko had won as a student while at Hosei University. It was presented to the Enighet Kendo Malmö after her death by her husband Kjell Lindberg.

Bank University). Ōsaki is listed in the *Judo Magazine* "Kendo Forum" as being 3-dan, which is a little confusing.[7] Professor Nagao was able to shed further light on this in a telephone conversation with Ōsaki-sensei, who explained that he had received *shodan* when he was a second-year student in junior high school. After that, he had been very busy studying and never had the chance to try for higher *dan* grades.

When he went to Britain, however, Takizawa bestowed upon him the grade of 3-dan considering his position as an instructor. He had complete confidence in this authorisation because of the excellent teachers he had formerly studied under. Thus, he responded that both (*shodan* and 3-dan) were in effect correct.

Incidentally, Ōsaki also mentioned to Professor Nagao that he respected Knutsen-sensei because his attitude was very sincere and humble, even though his instructor (Ōsaki) had a lower grade. Finally, Ōsaki emphasised that he never refused to try for *dan* grades. He is 5-dan now. He encourages his juniors to always strive for higher grades.

Following Horie, who had accompanied Knutsen to Sweden in June 1965, Knutsen then also took Ōsaki to Sweden in 1966 upon request from Robert von Sandor and together, they put von Sandor's students through an intense training schedule, "Paid for from our pockets and with some help

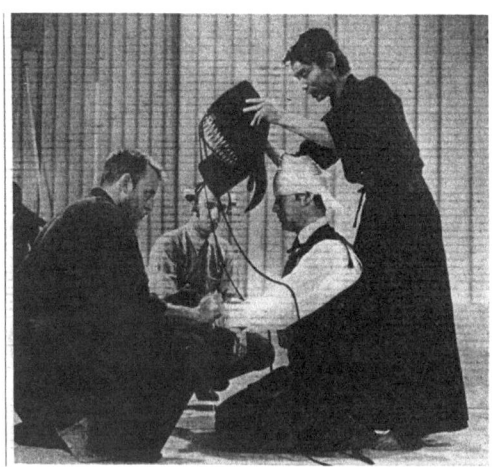

Roald Knutsen and Ōsaki assisting an actor putting on men for a TV programme. Circa 1966. Photo provided by Ōsaki-sensei via Professor Nagao.

---

7 Knutsen, Roald (Musashi), "Kendo Forum". *In Judo Magazine*. Croyden, Surrey: Judo Limited, January 1968, p23.

from BKA funds, small as they were." A letter to Lidstone from Knutsen in 1968 states that kendo in Sweden under the leadership and guidance of von Sandor—a highly motivated and self-confessed Japanophile—had gone from strength to strength. Active kendo clubs were listed in Gothenburg, Karlskrona, Karlstad, Helsingborg, Norrköping, and Stockholm.

Von Sandor had enlisted the support of Watanabe Akio (5-dan) who was living in Copenhagen. He commuted to Helsingborg to teach at the club there. Other Japanese sensei were installed in the clubs in Gothenburg (Nakai, 5-dan), Karlstad, and Karlskrona. Von Sandor himself was active in Stockholm at three clubs: University Kendo Club, Southern Stockholm Kendo Club, and his own Yamashi Kendo Dojo. He was joined by Watanabe Akio after moving to Stockholm.

In 1968, Hanshi 9-dan Ozawa Takashi toured Europe including England, and returning visitor in 1969 was Takizawa Kōzō who led an official delegation from Japan to discuss the European Kendo Federation/Oshu Kendo Renmei. Indeed, the UK and Europe were blessed by the attention they were getting in Japan in those early days, or so it seemed. As kendo became more organised in Europe, however, stress fractures started to appear in the most unlikely places. It is time now to turn our attention to the politics of early European kendo.

Hanshi Takizawa Kōzō

Hanshi 9-dan Ozawa Takashi in St James' Park, London, with R.A. Lidstone, 1968

CHAPTER 4

Genesis of the European Kendo Renmei

Following the establishment of the BKA in 1962, Roald Knutsen was contacted by a Hungarian Count Robert von Sandor. Von Sandor, a resident of Sweden, had been directly referred to Knutsen by Ōya Kazuo. Correspondence started with many letters followed by visits from both parties to Sweden, the UK, and various places in Europe. Discussions took place about spreading kendo in Europe, and sowing the seeds for an overseeing body which would become the European Kendo Renmei (EKR). Knutsen preferred to call it Ōshu Kendo Renmei.

> "Contact with von Sandor occurred sometime in 1961 or 1962; Robert von Sandor had contacted the AJKF by letter, requesting help for his kendo starters in Stockholm and was referred to us as we might help him. In the meantime, we received a letter from Ōya Kazuo-sensei (Hanshi 8-dan), the Secretary-General of the AJKF (also becoming a staunch supporter of our embryonic efforts), telling us of von Sandor's contact. It was at this point, I recall, that Arai-sensei also introduced himself to us, encouraged to do so by Yuno-sensei, Ōya-sensei, and Ozawa Takashi-sensei (Hanshi 9-dan)." (Knutsen)

As mentioned in the previous chapter, Knutsen had first been invited by von Sandor to go to Sweden in the summer of 1962, where he spent a week or more instructing the locals. He would subsequently visit Sweden several times as kendo later spread to Malmo in the south thanks to Horie Etsuko. In the winter of 1966, Knutsen went to Stockholm again with his young Japanese friend, Ōsaki Shintarō. The kendo fraternity was growing, and those who could teach kendo were greatly welcomed by hankering beginners.

In June 1964, a final agreement on the formal founding of the "European Group" was reached. R.A. Lidstone, Robert von Sandor, and Roald and Patricia Knutsen established the European Kendo Renmei (also known as the Ōshū Kendo Renmei) at the end of that year. However, the proposed statutes of the European Kendo Renmei would not formally be written and released until 1966, and this group would remain what was essentially an interim organisation until the official inauguration of the European Kendo Federation in 1970.

The first official general meeting of the EKR was not held until November 1968 in Leicester, England. Count Robert von Sandor was appointed president and the Knutsens served as secretary and treasurer. References to both the Ōshū Kendo Renmei and the European Kendo Renmei continued to be used until Knutsen resigned from the organisation in 1969, although he would continue to represent the interests of the British Kendo Association until 1970. He had produced the official EKR letterhead first used in a letter to Lidstone on May 27, 1966.

The periodical *Judo Magazine* ran regular articles and a kendo forum from the early 60s through to 1974. In a 1965 issue of the magazine, it was stated that the countries chiefly concerned with kendo promotion at the time after the UK

Letterhead from records of the time (Author's collection)

were Sweden, West Germany and Yugoslavia (referred to as the Jugoslav Kendo Community).[1]

By this time, however, first contact with groups in France, Belgium, Holland, Germany, and Morocco had been established, which were followed by collective practices. Each group was self-financed, but small administration costs for the first two years were covered by the Knutsens, and from whatever small funding was available from the BKA.

In the case of Belgium, Jacques Dupont had become interested in kendo after reading R. A. Lidstone's book (1964). Dupont contacted Lidstone directly, who in turn introduced him to Knutsen. Letters between the two were exchanged on a regular basis from early in 1966. This culminated in a visit by Roald Knutsen and Mike Tucker from the BKA to the Yama Arashi Dojo in Brussels from September 22–26 that year for training and a grading. Jacques Dupont was keen for kendo to become fully established in Belgium, and to also be a part of the EKR. They subsequently became affiliated members in 1967.[2] A letter dated March 16, 1966, from Knutsen to R.A. Lidstone paints a realistic picture of what kendo must have been like in these fledgling countries:

> "Our contact with Mr. Dupont in Belgium is rapidly becoming closer, and he is most enthusiastic to establish proper kendo there. Von Sandor has invited him to Sweden during my visit in mid-June, and maybe he will make it. If not, I have arranged for Jock to go to Brussels in September for ten days of kendo training. Looking at the photograph Mr. Dupont has sent me, they appear to be about the stage we were after a couple of years back in 1959 or so. Not too brilliant, but plenty of enthusiasm."

Further meetings and correspondence between representatives from Holland,

---

1 "*Kendo Forum*". In Judo Magazine IX N4. Croydon, Surrey: Judo Limited, January 1965, p 15.
2 L'Aminot, Tanguy, *L'Histoire du Kendo en France*. Accessed May 2016. http://chaken.fr/articlehistoire.html

including J.H. Odinot and A.B. Pruis, editor of a Dutch karate magazine, G. Stobbaerts of the Budo Club du Maroc, and Dr. Durix of Casablanca, as well as kendoka from Switzerland and France took place. According to a report by Roald Knutsen, the first gathering of the small kendo groups existing in greater Europe was the one held in Brussels in January 1967. The meeting was attended by over 30 kendoka from all over Europe, and was held in the Yama Arashi Dojo under the auspices of the Association Belge d'Aikido, Kendo et Arts Martiaux (ABAKAM). They sought to establish further contact and expand the European Kendo Renmei. Several resident Japanese *dan* holders (*yūdansha*) were also present. They were to become known as the "unofficial advisory group", but more on that soon.

Yama Arashi Dojo 1967: From far left Friedhelm Dockendorf, unknown, Jacques Dupont talking with Robert von Sandor. Vaughn Williams, unknown

Kendo delegates came from Sweden, Holland, West Germany, France, Great Britain, and, of course, Belgium. Roald Knutsen led the British trio of himself, Cyril Chadwick (*shodan*, Bushi Budokai), and Vaughn Williams (5-kyū, Nenriki). Sweden was represented by the chairman of the European Kendo Renmei, Robert von Sandor (1-kyū), and Alan Ferner (3-kyū). Two delegates, Friedhelm Dockendorf (6-kyū, Cologne) and Eberhard Riemann (5-kyū, Wiesbaden) attended on West Germany's behalf. The Dutch contingent was headed by the well-known martial artist, Morioka Sengi, a judo 6-dan and high-ranked practitioner in aikido, karate, and kendo. With him was J.H. Odinot (4-kyū) and Pvan Swieten de Blom (6-kyū).

France sent four representatives headed by 5-dan Shiga Tadakatsu, a kendo graduate of the redoubtable Kokushikan University, winners of the 1966 All Japan University Kendo Championships (and many more since). His companions were

David Royer (6-kyū), R. Chartrain (6-kyū), and Vai The Duc (6-kyū) from South Vietnam. The host country made up the majority of kendoka who were led by Hokage Kotarō (2-dan) and Jacques Dupont (1-kyū).

According to Knutsen "The training schedule was very hard with five arduous sessions between Friday evening and Sunday afternoon. This was a very serious *kangeiko* (winter training), but was outstanding for the tremendous enthusiasm and friendship. I believe that full credit should go to Mr. Tony Thielemans (judo 3-dan) and aikido president of ABAKAM, and to Mr. Jacques Dupont for the

Yama Arashi Dojo 1967: From far left Roald Knutsen, Friedhelm Dockendorf, Morioka Sengi, Christian Colin, and Shiga Tadakatsu

smoothness and incredible organisation that was never obvious yet always there."

Throughout the *keiko* sessions, the strictest discipline was enforced by Roald Knutsen as the senior, and France-based Shiga devoted his considerable energies to every aspect of basic kendo training.

> "*Kakari-geiko* and *kirikaeshi* in proper Japanese style were the main fare. The *yudansha* were able to practise together several times as examples to the students, and were always active. These were often exciting bouts. On the last session with kendoka who camouflaged physical exhaustion remarkably well, two four-man teams fought a formal *shiai* that ended in a draw." (Knutsen)

About this time, Friedhelm Dockendorf, one of the leaders of the German group—a senior official in the German broadcasting service, Deutsche Rundfunk—suggested approaches might be made to invite the Shah of Iran to become president of the new federation. Shah Pahlavi had not then been deposed, but political upheaval was in wait. Nothing came of the suggestion other than an expression of interest. The Shah was about to enter an age of political unrest, but so was the newly formed EKR.

Yama Arashi Dojo 1967: Far right Friedhelm Dockendorf, Jacques Dupont talking with Robert von Sandor, far background centre Morioka Sengi, near centre Vaughn Williams

CHAPTER 5

The Bumpy Road from Renmei to Federation

```
European Kendo Renmei Executive
Chairman:   Count Robert von Sandor (Sweden)
Secretary:  Mr. Roald M. Knutsen (Great Britain)
Members:    Mr. R.A. Iddatone (Great Britain)
            Mr. Allan Turner (Sweden), Dagbergsvägen 2,
            Norrköping, Sweden
            Mr. Friedhelm Dockendorf (West Germany).
            Mr. Eberhard Riemann (West Germany)
            Mr. Jacques Dupont (Belgium)
Advisor:    Mr. Shintaro Osaki.
            Mr. Susumu Watanabe.
            Mr. Benjamin H. Hazard.
```

European Kendo Renmei executive list in 1967 from records of the time
(Author's collection)

Knutsen was invited to Japan by the AJKF as the European representative to take part in an individual goodwill competition in Japan in October, 1967. He was to attend a meeting with the AJKF. This took place in Tokyo and saw official recognition of the EKR and of European lower grades, and the supply of *menjo* and equipment was agreed upon.

An important part of the agenda was to try and establish an international governing body. The creation of an International Kendo Federation was unanimously agreed upon in principle, and the importance of Roald Knutsen's role in the discussions cannot be overstated. His brief had been quite simple: "To lay the foundations for a clearer and more positive relationship with Japan." He was an honest but shrewd negotiator, and this was acclaimed at the highest level by Kimura Tokutarō, president of the AJKF, and other officials. Nevertheless, the situation in Europe was becoming fractious, and resident Japanese experts were in the thick of it, as was the AJKF.

Coinciding with the formulation of the EKR in 1966, the loose association of five young Japanese teachers all in their twenties was a godsend. They were based in Europe and became an "unofficial advisory group" for European kendo. I have already mentioned them by name, but to remind the reader they were Watanabe Akio (Sweden, located in Copenhagen), Hokage Kotarō (Belgium, Pentax Cameras), Shiga Tadakatsu (France), Watanabe Susumu (Switzerland, UNESCO) and Fujii Okimitsu (UK, an English student in London). As the oldest member, Fujii was elected as leader of the group which met every few months to discuss how best they could help kendo in their respective countries. Morioka Sengi, who had lived in Europe (specifically Holland) the longest, also acted as an advisor from time to time.

Although the group was referred to as "unofficial", they were bestowed official AJKF recognition at a meeting in Brighton on September 14, 1969. This was where

Asa-geiko with 150 kendoka from 12 countries before the goodwill taikai on October 4, 1967, at the Nippon Budokan

The European Kendo Renmei

The following promotions within the *dan* degree ranks are announced by this Renmei:

To *Yon-dan* (4th *dan*):
  Mr. R. A. Lidstone (Nenriki Dojo)
  Mr. R. M. Knutsen (Butokukan Dojo)

To *Sandan* (3rd *dan*):
  Mr. J. Mathie (Saineikan Dojo)

Official consultations were conducted in Japan between representatives of the Z.N.K.R. and the Secretary-General of this Renmei regarding promotions in Europe and subject to ratification between the two parties all promotions made by this Renmei will be under the signatures of the Chairman together with five *hachidan sensei* in Japan. These rulings will be in operation until such time as revised rules are brought in by the new Kokusai Kendo Renmei. It must be clearly understood that only those rankings issued and authorised by the European Kendo Renmei have any validity in Europe.

EKR (Ōshū) Grading Announcement from 1967 (Author's collection)[1]

serious problems came to the fore. For one, some were surprised at the audacity of the Japanese governing body in designating their countrymen as leaders of foreign kendo. Delegates from six European countries sat down together: Sweden (Sandor), France (Hamot), Belgium (Dupont), Switzerland (Garlinski), Austria (Steiger) and Great Britain (Lidstone). Takizawa Kōzō represented the AJKF delegation, and Fujii Okimitsu was there on behalf of the "unofficial advisors". Von Sandor presided over the meeting as chairman of the EKR together with secretary Roald Knutsen as discussions were held to get the European group fully endorsed by the AJKF, albeit with a change of name, as the European Kendo Federation. The problem was, in the eyes of the Europeans, the preferential treatment afforded to the group of Japanese instructors who just happened to reside in Europe. Especially as some of them seemed to be taking things in a direction that others did not want.

---

1 "*Kendo Forum*". In *Judo Magazine* N2. Croydon, Surrey: Judo Limited, November 1967, p 17.

Nihon Kendo Kata
Ozawa Takashi with Roald Knutsen,
1968

THE BRITISH KENDŌ ASSOCIATION

COMMITTEE MEETING

10th June

Gentlemen,

We have the opportunity of meeting Mr. Robert von Sandor, Mr R.B. Odinot, Mr. S. van Swieten de Blom, Mr. S. Morioka, and Mr. Hokogi at the Nenriki Dōjō next Saturday and it has been proposed that we hold a special committee meeting of the Renmei together with these official representatives of three European Kendō communities so that we can generally get to know each other and discuss some of the wider issues of European Kendō.

Sir Frank Bowden, Vice-President of this Renmei, will also be present by our invitation.

Since the Dōjō is open that afternoon for general warm-up practice and it is expected that many Kendōka will take advantage of this, it is hoped that we can start this executive meeting with most members present at 4.30 PM. The meeting must end before 6.00 so that we can meet H.E. The Japanese Ambassador, Mr. Shima, and the other guests.

It is also suggested that all the yūdansha present attend including the Japanese guests. This does not include yūdansha from outside the sphere of this Renmei and that of the Z.N.K.R.

Yours sincerely,

Roald M. Knutsen,
Secretary,
The British Kendō Association.

2nd June, 1967

Notification from records of the time (Author's collection)

Knutsen, Shiga and Hokage. Circa 1968

As recorded in the "Kendo Forum" of Judo Magazine:[2]

"The Japanese Yudansha in Europe: These will form a special Advisory Group reorganised along lines drawn up by Mr. Hamot and presented to the General Meeting of the EKR shortly. The members of this A.G. will be authorised by the ZNKR (AJKF)."

Apprehensions had already been expressed about the actions of one of the prominent AG members in a letter from Knutsen to Takizawa Kōzō dated July 15, 1968: "The problem with Mr. Shiga is that his character and his general behaviour will be one that most deeply affects the EKR for the future. His influence in his resident country is very great."

The letter further states that this needs to be discussed with the AJKF the following year at the scheduled meeting in the UK. According to Knutsen, the greatest difficulty was Shiga and his unwillingness to accept advice or "conform to normal kendo relationships". According to Knutsen's assessment, he clearly intended to go his own way irrespective of whether it conflicted with the EKR or other combined Japanese opinion. He advised that in any official visit to the resident country of Shiga by high-ranking kendo sensei (i.e., France), care should be taken not to further augment his importance in the eyes of that country's kendoka.

His letter also pointed out that "proper kendo thinking and attitude" should be made clear to all of the members throughout Europe in the hope that they can understand the thinking of the EKR, however difficult this might be to achieve. He advised the AJKF to visit Sweden, the Netherlands, and England in particular because these other two countries "also adhered to proper kendo thinking and action."

Further conversations continued between the members of the EKR and Takizawa well into 1970. Knutsen pleaded with the AJKF. "It is a great pity that the actions of two or three mavericks should ruin the carefully built up relations we were beginning to enjoy with Japan." There was growing frustration with the official sanctioning by the AJKF of the "unofficial advisory group". "I must agree" states Knutsen, "with Robert von Sandor. It certainly looks as if the AJKF has supported the young Japanese while ignoring the people who run the various Renmei."

People including Benjamin Hazard, believed that the petitioning of the AJKF by the Europeans went unheeded as there was a "higher hidden agenda". Amongst those very firmly critical of the AJKF attitude and their actions was the influential

---

2 "*Kendo Forum*". In *Judo Magazine* Vol XIV No 4. Croydon, Surrey: Judo Limited, October 1969, p.28

International Businessmen's Kendo Renmei, which would also continue to support the Eikoku Kendo Renmei after the split within the BKA in 1973. According to Knutsen, support continued with acceptance of EKR members to stay and study in Japan as well as receiving visits from teachers and recommendations for grade promotion.

There is some written evidence of these tensions, and the concerns existing between senior members of the EKR (notably Roald Knutsen and Robert von Sandor). Von Sandor took issue in respect to communications between senior Japanese officials and Europe. He clearly expressed that, in his opinion, certain senior members of the AJKF had little respect for the European kendo leaders, and were set on bypassing them in preference for the AG. They would issue specific instructions and directives for European kendo, but the federation was never informed. Von Sandor wrote personally to the AKJF expressing his concerns about being cut out of the loop, and the need for these issues to be addressed. He confided in Knutsen:

```
Neither ZNKR or Mr Takizawa take any notice of the existence of the
President of Oshu Kendo Renmei.
It seems to me that the japanese authority liked establish contact only
with japanese kendoka in Europa (see also copy of Mr Knutsen's letter
to Mr Fuji). It means that the organisation problem on the national
field is in the hand of the japanese teachers in Europa.

Takizawa-senseis explanation to you, that he could not write to me
because he do not know my address is very peculiar since the letter
in which he wrote this was addressed to you c/o my name and personal
address.

The concusion must be that ZNKR do not like deal with european kendo leaders
and that they look at us as people not worthy to put reliance on.

They determine over our head and give order to japanese kendoka to do
the organisation. Why should then the european kendo leaders take the
job, responsibility and solve the economical problems?

We the leaders in England and Sweden are just ordinary kendoka and as
true bushi we shall attend to our own kendo practice and do not care
about organisation, development and solving of "polètical problems"

The japanese gentleman who have establisht all this problem can take
over all the responsibility since they seems to have the whole confidence
of the ZNKR.
```

An extract of a letter from von Sandor to Knutsen (Author's collection)

By this stage some of the advisory group had already returned to Japan as their work contracts had ended. Hokage Kōtarō was presented with a Napoleonic sword when he left as a token of gratitude for his support; he had been in Belgium since 1966 and had helped a great deal with their development. Eventually, the remainder of the group retreated into the comfort of their host country's organisations to assist as best they could on a more personal level during the early 1970s, but the twilight years of the 60s was treacherous ground for everybody. Undoubtedly all concerned had the best interests of kendo in their minds, but the "Japan versus the rest" ruffled many local feathers.

Looking back and considering both time and circumstance, it is not difficult to imagine the buoyant exuberance of this group in that they were the *crème de la crème* of the then European kendo world slowly emerging from the dust of a previous era. To be treated and regarded as an expert, almost a "kendo god", could have easily given delusions of grandeur to these young and impressible *yūdansha*. It should be remembered that not all of them let it go to their heads. Time will be the judge of how some of them acted, what they achieved, and if they will be remembered in the same light as the founding Europeans in this tale of two cultures.

The pioneers of the EKR trusted Japan, and entertained a strong feeling of hope. Reciprocation, however seems to have fallen short, resulting in a hesitant mistrust that continued for many decades. Such a failure of confidence and breakdown in communication appears to be at loggerheads with the amount of early support that was heaped upon the BKA and the EKR. This was undoubtedly due to the actions of a few individuals who had the ear of the Japanese authorities.

It is worth studying the remarks made in a *Judo Magazine* article, on the visit to England of Hanshi 9-dan Koshikawa Hidenosuke in 1964. He described kendo in the world as having only "one head". "That is, the Zen Nippon Kendo Renmei, and any conflicting politics had no place in kendo. The strength of kendo lies in its unity."[3] He pledged the full support of the AJKF to the growth of the European Kendo Renmei. Strong words indeed, sincerely put by one of the most senior figures at the time. Unfortunately, "unity" was compromised, and politics were to have impeding consequences for the smooth development of kendo in Europe.

---

3 "*Kendo Forum*". In *Judo Magazine* N4. Croydon, Surrey: Judo Limited, January 1965, p 15.

CHAPTER 6

Across the Channel, Kendo in France

One country that underwent a particularly topsy-turvy road to unity was France. In Paris on April 28, 1970, the 1st General Assembly of the European Kendo Federation was convened and the use of the term EKR was stopped. Delegates were unanimous in their conviction that this AJKF sanctioned "Advisory Group" should only act under the full control of the Executive Board of the EKF. It would appear that this was not acceptable to the Japanese AG members. This exacerbated tensions between the French kendo body headed by Shiga (FKR), and the rest of the EKF. There was a distinct nonconformist attitude towards the EKR and then later with the EKF with regard to the policies they were attempting to implement. "In our own direction" was the order coming from FKR and Shiga. This sentiment had apparently built up over several years. While the advisory group considered their good intentions to be collective and in the interest of all European member countries, they came across as perhaps too unilateral for the FKR. They had their own programme for kendo in France led by Shiga, and would not be influenced by external interference, especially coming from within Europe.

Hokage Kōtarō at Nenriki Dojo, 1969

Kendo had floundered in its infancy in France after an earlier introduction by Jim Alcheik, the first foreign student of Mochizuki Minoru of the Yoseikan in Japan. On his return to France, Alcheik founded the French Federation of Aikido, Taijutsu, and Kendo (FFATK) in 1955, and opened a dojo in the Avenue Parmentier in Paris called the Mochizuki Club in 1958. Kendo did not occupy the top spot in Alcheik's teaching curriculum, but he was the first to introduce it in France on a continuous basis. Alcheik also presented kendo to a wider audience by organising demonstrations in Paris and the provinces, and creating a "Gala of Martial Arts" at the Salle Wagram in Paris, starting on April 3, 1959. After demonstrations of judo and karate, the event ended with the first championship of kendo in France, albeit with few participants.[1] Alcheik defeated his own student Cocatre, but was then beaten in the final by Jacques Levy who became the "first" champion of kendo in France.

Jim Alcheik 1960

This event is followed by another on April 1, 1960. The guest of honour was none other than Anton Geesink, European Judo champion and future world and Olympic champion. Nearly a thousand people attended and watched Nguyen Van Nam become the kendo champion this year. These two events really mark the start of kendo in France. Unfortunately, Alcheik, who was reputedly a French secret service agent, died in an explosion in Algeria known as the Villa El Biard Incident of 1962. His death and disappearance from the martial arts world in France would halt the spread of kendo.

Without a shadow of a doubt, the arrival of Shiga greatly enhanced the structure and early progression of his host country's kendo. Shiga then took full control of the FKR, and it became commonly known as the "French Shiga Kendo Federation", much to the chagrin of the EKR executive members at the time. His initial involvement was met with excitement at the prospect of another high-graded practitioner being resident in Europe. Shiga had been introduced to Alain Floquet[2] through a mutual Japanese friend who was a karate student of Aikido-Yoseikan and karate sections of the Association Sportive de la Préfecture de Police de Paris'.[3]

According to Floquet, "In 1966, I entrusted the karate section to a young policeman colleague (Roger Paschy) and I created the kendo section of the Police de Paris." Shiga was working in a Japanese restaurant in Paris having arrived in France in 1965. As one of the co-founders of the FKR, Floquet saw in Shiga the ability to stimulate kendo in France. He offered him the opportunity to teach kendo in the clubs where Floquet also taught aikido. Shiga readily accepted. He also tried to reach out to the youth, and a few dozen children quickly took on this new discipline.

On June 15, 1969, Claude Hamot, the new president of the FKR, was enthusiastic at the growth of kendo seen in France. The fact that the number of entries

---

1 L'Aminot, Tanguy, *L'Histoire du Kendo en France*. Accessed May 2016. http://chaken.fr/articlehistoire.html

2 Alain Floquet was an aikido sensei, and a former student of Jim Alcheik. He was also the founder of l'Aikibudo and a 9-dan Hanshi, CERA (Circle of Studies and Research on Aikido in France).

3 Minoru Mochizuki had introduced Aikido to France around 1950 through his organisation Yoseikan based in Shizuoka.

selected for the third annual tournament was double that of the previous year with some 40 people taking part was cause for optimism. Successful *dan* promotions indicated just how well the management was progressing. The number of French *yūdansha* increased: six went to *shodan* and four went to 2-dan in 1969.[4] Under the direction of Shiga, the level of expertise in France rose quickly to match that of the other countries within the EKR. Sadly, the early euphoria attached to these achievements was not to last.

Japanese delegation in Paris 1969. Far left standing Jean-Claude Tuvi, next in front of tall person Claude Hamot and Andre Tuvi, seated second row second from Claude Hamot, Shiga Tadakatsu

A very rare gathering of the rival factions after a combined keiko: 1 Shiga Tadakatsu, 2 Alain Floquet, 3 Bernard Durand and Yoshimura Ken'ichi.

---

4 L'Aminot, Tanguy, *L'Histoire du Kendo en France*. Accessed May 2016. http://chaken.fr/articlehistoire.html

Eventually, the rather extreme personality of Shiga would contribute to a division within France's kendo organisation itself, and at the end of 1970 a split occurred. Some officers of the FKR, including Claude Hamot and several young practitioners left Shiga's organisation and joined another, the FFK with Jean-Pierre Niay. It is unclear exactly why the split occurred because those around at that time are quite reserved with their recollections. It seems that the personality of Shiga played a big role in this matter, but it is also likely that domestic issues and personality clashes were the root of discord as well.

This rival organisation—previously started in 1955 by Alcheik but mothballed due to the presence of the FKR—was resurrected by Yoshimura Ken'ichi. He was a 4-dan graduate of the prestigious University of Tokyo, and had arrived in February 1970 to spend a year in France. Coincidently, Claude Hamot, as president of the FKR, had made contact with Takizawa Kōzō-sensei because of Shiga's extreme personality in 1969 to replace Shiga with another expert.

Few Japanese delegations from the AJKF hitherto had appreciated the efforts of Shiga, nor were they particularly predisposed to his personality. The Japanese government, knowing that Yoshimura had arrived in France and of his passion for kendo, also asked him to assist further in the development process by remaining in France.

The remaining leaders of the FKR were probably not too concerned about the dissent of some 20 members and the presence of this young Japanese teacher. After all, the FKR was the body affiliated with the AJKF and the EKF. This had been clearly established in Paris in 1970 when the EKR was rebranded as the EKF. One can only imagine how difficult the situation must have been for this young man Yoshimura, being in the middle of a tense situation centred on a Japanese technical advisor who was older and more experienced than himself. However, it would appear that Shiga and his qualification of 5-dan was at least questionable, especially as it later transpired that his 3-dan *menjo* had allegedly been tampered with.

On June 6, 1971, the FKR organised the annual French championship with 37 participants in the presence of 7-dan Kumada-sensei, who was an observer from the AJKF. In the report published by the French *Budo* magazine in October, the FKR also stated that they had been visited by four delegates from the AJKF that year, including the preeminent teachers Kasahara, Ogawa, and Ono.[5]

Budo also published an account by Yoshimura of the "French Championship" convened by the FFK, which took place on June 20, and saw 18 participants take part.[6] France, therefore, had two champions of kendo that year. Pierre Martin, 3-dan, for the FKR, and Bernard Durand, also 3-dan, for the FFK. The FFK also held demonstrations and workshops, but their activities did not seem to bother the FKR due to their status as the "official organisation".

---

5 Ibid
6 Ibid

In July 1972, *Judo Journal* announced the "formalisation of kendo" in France, and the birth of the National Kendo Committee (CNK).[7] In November that year, however, the FKR leaders discovered to their surprise that it was the FFK who had won recognition from the powerful French Judo Federation and Associated Disciplines (FFJDA), which in the early 1960s was the goal of all kendo members.[8]

Actually, in the official bulletin of the "French Federation of Judo and Jujitsu" and "Quorum of Black Belts" there was a notification from Jim Alcheik in 1961 showing that his FFATK had been recognised within the FFJDA, meaning that kendo became a discipline associated with judo when the FFK was operational in the early days. The death of Alcheik had essentially meant the end this association, but the precedent and history was certainly there.

The FKR had the same ambitions, and in 1968 presented a protocol to integrate kendo within the judo federation. The FFJDA, after studying the project, provided venues and official promotion for kendo. It was thus with great surprise that members of the FKR learned "a section for kendo" had emerged in the FFJDA with Yoshimura as the technical advisor, and that he was preparing the selection of a French team for the 2nd World Kendo Championships planned for Los Angeles in 1973.

On November 27, a director of the FKR sent a letter to the FFJDA expressing their intense disappointment at this turn of events. It mentions that candidates selected by the FKR to participate in the European Championship in Stockholm in 1972 had been disallowed without reason, and those proposed for the world championships would also not be permitted to participate.

What had happened? Having had contact with Mr. Kimura (President of the International Kendo Federation), Mr. Kasahara (Secretary General of the IKF), and Robert von Sandor (Chairman of the EKF), the FFJDA decided at its AGM on May 7, 1972, to create an official kendo section (CNK) independent to the FKR. According to *L' Histoire du kendo en France*, there were external pressures. It may have been quite simply that the position of the AJKF and the EKR had not been made clear on the issues of support in respect of the FKR and the CNK before the announcement.

Whatever the case, this turn of events was to cause much ill feeling between the two rival groups, especially regarding grade representation after the CNK was authorised by the all-powerful FFJDA.[9] It would take nearly three years to ease the tensions in what would be an ongoing state of turmoil.

Following the establishment of the CNK, this new organisation went from strength to strength under the guidance of Yoshimura Ken'ichi. Shiga and his organisation (the FKR) would gradually disappear. Although ousted, and without

---

7 Ibid
8 Ibid
9 Ibid

any sanctioned responsibility, the FKR still tried to extend its activities for some time, especially in seeking parity with the CNK within the FFJDA.

If individual members of the CNK, such as Claude Hamot, were open to discussion and reintegration, others were not. The CNK quickly rewrote the history of kendo in France. Early forays in kendo dating back to 1955 were disregarded, and officially it all started [properly] in 1973.

In April 1974, a letter addressed the issue of the integration of the FKR into the CNK. The question of the validity of *dan* grades was addressed again. This was a burning issue that concerned both the FKR and FFK back in the day, as members of the latter took their grades with them when it became the CNK. The first *dan* grades were granted by the Japanese either by roving delegations or during the 1st World Kendo Championships. Grades were also previously awarded in France following European events, and confirmed by the EKR after consultation with senior figures such as Roald Knutsen when he had visited Paris in February 1968.[10] In other words, FKR member grades were legit.

Now, this did not seem to matter, and grades held by FKR members were relegated to having no value at all. FKR members were also unable to participate in international events and felt betrayed by both the Japanese and European federations. Some FKR members gave in and joined the CNK after a few years, but many remained disillusioned and quit practising kendo. Alain Floquet resumed aikido and founded CERA (Circle of Studies and Research on Aikido) rather than continuing the uphill struggle to achieve the unification of the two groups.

Shiga Tadakatsu disappeared entirely from kendo. There was some speculation that he may have stayed in France working as a cook, although this cannot be verified. An appearance as an actor in *Le saut de l'ange* (1971) is also mentioned but nothing after.[11] According to Alain Floquet, however, he returned to Japan after 1973. He did apparently make visits to France later on but did not involve himself in kendo there ever again.

---

10 "*Kendo Forum*". In *Judo Magazine* N7. Croydon, Surrey: Judo Limited, April 1968, p 18.
11 IMDb. Accessed May 2016. http://www.imdb.com/title/tt0067710/

CHAPTER 7

A Parting of the 'Ways'

What of the EKF and its founding as these events unfolded? In 1969, Roald Knutsen resigned as Secretary-General of the Ōshū Kendo Renmei stating "As I recall, the growing commitment to kendo here became pressing and I resigned from the Secretaryship of the Ōshū Kendo Renmei on an entirely amicable basis." From an "official" point of view, EKR had been well established with a full constitution, proper bank account, and audited finances. Patricia Knutsen served as Honorary Treasurer to both the BKA until 1973, and the EKR until 1969—when everything was passed over to Robert von Sandor.

Von Sandor continued as chairman of the EKF after his election in Paris in 1970 at the first General Assembly. He remained in that post until 1982, after which he became Honorary President of the EKF and a new chapter began.

Interestingly, as early as 1967 a report in the "Kendo Forum" of *Judo Magazine* states that "In Europe there are eight countries united under the European Kendo Renmei, and of these eight only one shows divisions—England."[1] These divisions had actually started as early as 1960 according to correspondence between Knutsen and Lidstone. This eventually led to a major schism between British kendo enthusiasts in 1973, culminating in Roald Knutsen resigning from the BKA. In its simplest form, it was the result of differences of opinion and personality clashes.

Ian Parker-Dodd[2] offered a tentative hypothesis as to how governing bodies in sport develop during discussions with colleagues about the evolution of sport and its governance. Rugby was one sport that was discussed because of the union/league split, and also the split of diving from the amateur swimming association.

One point of view put forward was a business theory about pioneers, diversification and management development. The perception was that sport does not follow such trends and Ian observed that the development of sporting bodies goes through the following stages:

> "One or two charismatic personalities start off and the activity then thrives on a wave of sustained enthusiasm; as numbers grow the small group of people around the founders then behave as if they were oligarchs or satraps and start fighting amongst each other for 'territory'."

At this point, an organisation quite often splinters and sometimes disappears. If an organisation comes through this period successfully, it develops a functioning democracy with a suitable bureaucracy; if it doesn't do this then it just stumbles on, going through and just surviving crisis after crisis.

---

1 "*Kendo Forum*". In *Judo Magazine* X1. Croydon, Surrey: Judo Limited, February 1967.
2 Ian Parker-Dodd is a retired Senior Lecturer, MA (Oxon) Dip.Ed (Oxon). University of Gloucestershire School of Sport, England. He is a kendo 5-dan and founded the Gloucestershire University Kendo club in 1994. He was National Coach, National Referee, Chair of the British Kendo Association Coaching Board from 2006-2008, and British Kendo team manager from 1994 to 1998.

The events of 1973 and the schism within the BKA can be pretty much attributed to this theory. As early as 1958 the personalities of the initial group of members had clashed, not between Knutsen and Lidstone though, but by others who had joined the Shinto Ryu at the London Judo Society. Rival factions were established by returning members who had spent time in Japan. Tensions reached the point where expulsions were made from the organisation; these would later be overturned but the damage was already done. 'Vendetta' would be the name of the next game. Following the death of Lidstone , Knutsen found it harder to maintain control and appeared to some as dictatorial in his behaviour. With Lidstone gone a power vacuum opened. Knutsen became isolated, and family and business matters, together with being based in Brighton, perhaps added to the problems. Alliances were formed at the Nenriki Dojo in London and these would be the 'new order' which would lead to a head-on confrontation resulting in the resignation and departure of Roald Knutsen in 1973.

This was, however, much more clear cut for the AJKF, IKF, and EKF than the scenario they had experienced in France, and it presented a far less complex problem. Not a split or a rival organisation, just the resignation of one individual. The status quo was then maintained without issue.

Following his resignation, Roald Knutsen formed a new kendo group called the BKR or British Kendo Renmei with the aim of providing an alternative choice for kendo students who were more interested in practising and developing their understanding of the traditional arts and ways of Japanese martial culture rather than treating kendo primarily as a competitive sport.

The BKA remains as the governing body for kendo, iaido and jodo and is recognised by the AJKF as founder members of the European and International Kendo Federations. Its stated objectives are to foster and develop the practice and spirit of kendo, iaido and jodo on traditional lines; to organise, regulate and promote on a national and international basis; to represent the UK internationally; and to regulate the promotion of members to higher degrees. The BKR, the Dai Nippon Butokukai, and various other independent groups continue to follow similar objectives under their own autonomy.

European Goodwill Taikai, London 1973. Notable BKA members after "the schism" together with French members of the newly formed CNK. The AJKF/IKF is represented by Kasahara-sensei

CHAPTER 8

The Inaugural European Kendo Tournaments

There is some dispute as to exactly when the first "official" European Kendo Championships took place, but my opinion is that it was held in Paris on May 5, 1968, and organised by "la France Kendo Renmei" (FKR) under the patronage of the Ōshū Kendo Renmei. The name is recorded on the flyer for the event below as the "First European Kendo Tournament" held at the Gymnase on Boulevard Blanqui. It was agreed by those representatives present on the previous day from Austria, Belgium, Great Britain, Holland, Switzerland and France who had all practised together at the Gymnase du Stade Francais that the winner of this competition would be declared the "European Kendo Champion". It is not clear, however as the records do not confirm if this was the same venue as where the tournament was held. The competition was an individual event only. It had been originally planned to hold a team event as well, but this never transpired.

> "Charles Lidstone (R.A.), Chairman of the British Kendo Association was elected President of the Tournament and Louis Lasselin (President of the French Kendo Renmei) as Vice President. The Japanese *yudansha* (unofficial advisory group) from France, Switzerland, Belgium and Great Britain very kindly offered to form the judging panel, under the Presidency of Mr. Morioka from Holland. Their offer was gladly accepted."[1]

The Results—1st Place Bernard Durand (France); 2nd Place Roald Knutsen (GB); 3rd Place Gaston Sterckx (Belgium) and Claude Hamot (France)

Hamot received a special award for "Kendo Technique", and Cyril Chadwick (GB) an award for what I assume was "Fighting Spirit" but referred to as "Kendo Spirit". It was presented by Patricia Knutsen.

Following the event in Paris, in the same year (1968) on November 2, the BKA Yudansha Taikai (Inaugural Taikai for the Japan Airlines Cup), was held in Coalville, Leicestershire, at Bujutsukai West End. Bujutsukai West End is listed in the register of the British Kendo Association. In 1968, there were 18 dojo/clubs in existence in the UK. The following day was the first official meeting of the EKR, which was solely for the discussion and approval of the federation's statutes that had been formulated two years previously.

The results of the Yudansha Taikai in Leicester were—1st Place Victor Cook (GB); 2nd Place Bernard Durand (France); 3rd Place Brian Hilliard (GB)

On September 14, 1969, an official meeting of the EKR took place at Nenriki in London. The official BKA representatives present are listed as Mr. R.A. Lidstone (Chairman) and Mr. J Clarke (Executive Member). In a report from the To-Ken Society it states that the event was organised under the auspices of the EKR as a Taikai in honour of the official delegation from the AJKF. The delegation was

---

1 Lidstone, R.A. "The Fencing Master". In *Journal of the British Academy of Fencing* Vol.3 No.5. Cheam, Surrey: The British Academy of Fencing, July 27, 1968, p 2.

FRANCE KENDO RENMEI
Affiliée à la ZEN NIPPON KENDO RENMEI

△ △ △ △ △ △ △

PREMIER TOURNOI EUROPEEN DE KENDO
avec la participation des équipes de :

AUTRICHE BELGIQUE GRANDE-BRETAGNE
PAYS-BAS SUISSE FRANCE ET DE 10
EXPERTS JAPONAIS.

DIMANCHE 5 MAI 1968
à 14 heures
GYMNASE du BOULEVARD BLANQUI — Paris 13e

▽ ▽ ▽ ▽ ▽ ▽ ▽

COMPETITIONS INDIVIDUELLES
COMPETITIONS par EQUIPES NATIONALES
DEMONSTRATIONS par Maitres et Experts Japonais

TOURNOI organisé par la France Kendo Renmei sous le patronnage de la OSHU KENDO Renmei et avec la participation:

LA REVUE DES ARTS MARTIAUX
37 rue de la Belle Feuille
92 - BOULOGNE . Tel: 408-12-46

Original flyer

comprised of five 8-dan, three of whom were Hanshi, and one Kyōshi 7-dan.[2]

According to the report, on the big day the Europeans did their utmost to show their best kendo to the visiting experts from Japan, and that all the bouts throughout the day, as well as the various demonstrations, were superb to watch. The event was even attended by Prince Tomohito, with Sir Frank Bowden giving a welcome address to the Japanese guests and members of the various European dojo taking

---
[2] The To-Ken Society of Great Britain. *Programme 5*. October 6, 1969, p 3.

part. Takizawa Kōzō, chief representative of the delegation, replied to this in Japanese with a translation read out by Roald Knutsen. R.A. Lidstone, Chairman of the BKA also gave a speech that was interpreted into Japanese by Fujii Okimitsu.

```
DŌJŌ IN BRITAIN.

    Kendō development in Britain is motivated, not by a desire for great
numbers; this is something that does not matter to Kendoka; but we want
to establish a select number of Dōjō in a network to cover the main areas
of the country.  Kendō restarted in this country in 1958, after a longish
break from 1940, when the original Dōjō was bombed out.  In the past four
years, a number of excellent groups have formed and these are detailed
below:-

         DŌJŌ NAME                  LOCATION
         BUDOKAN.                   MIDDLESBROUGH, YORKSHIRE.

         BUJUTSUKAI.                BLYTH, NORTHUMBERLAND.


  DOJO NAME                    LOCATION

  BUJUTSUKAI WEST END.         COALVILLE, LEICESTERSHIRE.
  BUSHI BUDOKAI.               PORTSMOUTH, HAMPSHIRE.
  BUTOKUKAN.                   BRIGHTON, SUSSEX.
  FLEETWOOD.                   FLEETWOOD, LANCASHIRE.
  LANCASTER.                   LANCASTER.
  LEICESTER.                   LEICESTER.
  LLANGOLLEN.                  LLANGOLLEN, DENBIGHSHIRE.
  NENRIKI.                     SOUTHWARK, LONDON.
  NEWPORT.                     NEWPORT, MONMOUTHSHIRE.
  NORWICH.                     NORWICH, NORFOLK.
  READING.                     READING, BERKSHIRE.
  SUDBURY.                     SUDBURY, SUFFOLK.
  UNIVERSITY OF SUSSEX.        FALMER, SUSSEX.
  WREXHAM.                     WREXHAM, DENBIGHSHIRE.
  ZANSHIN.                     BRISTOL.
  JUDOKAI                      BURTON-UPON-TRENT, STAFFORDSHIRE.
```

BKA Dojo list from records of the time (Author's collection)

Hanshi 8-dan Takizawa Kōzō and Hanshi 8-dan Ueda Hajime gave the first demonstration of the Nihon Kendo Kata. "The strict form of these movements was not conducted at great speed but were obviously performed with great attention to style and were very beautiful to watch, like living Japanese Prints." The first rounds were followed by the semi-finals and finals of both the kyū and dan-grade Japan Airlines Yudansha tournaments.

The 2nd Japan Airlines Yudansha Tournament at Nenriki, London. September 13, 1969. Jock Hopson striking men

From far left, Roald Knutsen sitting next to R.A. Lidstone (possibly one of the last images before his death in November the same year), John Clarke. 1969

From far right, Robert von Sandor (back to camera), Jean-Claude Tuvi, Claude Hamot, André Tuvi, Jacques Dupont, Mr. Delbauve, John Clarke, R A Lidstone. 1969

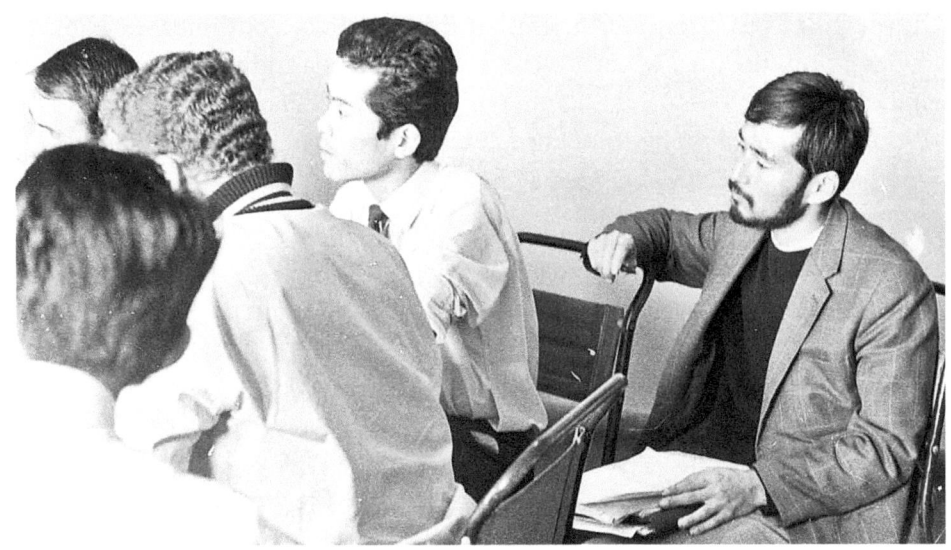

Shiga Tadakatsu (far right) Fujii Okimitsu (front). 1969

From left, Victor Cook, Hanshi 8-dan Nakakura Kiyoshi, Kyōshi 7-dan Iho Kiyotsugu. 1969

```
The Japanese Party.

This will be composed as follows:-

Head of Party:   Takizawa Kozo        Hanshi, 8th dan    (Tokyo)
Member:          Nakakura Kyoshi         "         "     (Tokyo)
                 Ueda Hajime             "         "     (Kagawa)
                 Sakuma Saburo        Kyoshi       "     (Tokyo)
                 Iho Kiyotsugu           "         "     (Tokyo)
                 Sato Shiro              "      7th dan  (Hyogo)
```

Notification of the attending Japanese party, from records of the time
(Author's collection)

Throughout the afternoon, these battling kendoka continued to eliminate each other until the final winners were revealed as a kenshi from Switzerland, Mr. Galjnski, another from London, and a girl also from London. I believe these are the results of the kyū-grade competition, but unfortunately I have been unable to locate the results of the *yūdansha* matches.

Hanshi 8-dan Takizawa Kōzō- and Hanshi 8-dan Ueda Hajime – Kendo kata

Hanshi 8-dan Takizawa Kōzō- and Hanshi 8-dan Ueda Hajime – Nanahonme

It was also mentioned how Hanshi 8-dan Nakakura Kiyoshi later gave a demonstration of *iai-jutsu*, which was deemed to be "fantastic". As the report describes the scene, "For those who are familiar with the film *Seven Samurai*, this was the expert swordsman coming to life. His total composure relaxation and calm facial expression as he sat quietly before bursting into each movement was said to be incredible." The author was clearly moved by the performance. "Bursting is the wrong word—it was more a slow unwinding, almost a reluctance to draw the sword rapidly accelerating to a crescendo of straight clear cut movements ending in a lightning return of the sword to the scabbard." Performed without a sound or rattle with the sword returned to the scabbard without even an exhalation of breath, was defined by the writer as: "The only sound that was audible was the whistle of the blade through the air."

A demonstration of Gogyō-no-Kata, old kendo forms, was also conducted by

Kyōshi 8-dan Iho Kiyotsugu and Kyōshi 8-dan Sakuma Saburo using *bokutō*. "Short, rhythmic patterns of movement, not dissimilar to the forms of the Nihon Kendo Kata." The six members of the delegation gave the final demonstration in pairs and performed matches against each other. "To the non-expert, it might have appeared to be more about fencing than in the earlier European competitive bouts, with the movements quicker but more controlled, as might be expected. The noise was just as loud, but sounding somewhat more Japanese! The last match showed that kendo was not without its humorous side when one sensei repeatedly struck rapid blows to the head of his opponent with apparently funny remarks and much laughter."

Hanshi 8-dan Nakakura Kiyoshi

Hanshi 8-dan Nakakura Kiyoshi

On September 16, the delegation then travelled on to France, Sweden, Holland, Switzerland, and Italy before returning to Japan on September 30. Another tournament notice was sent out to European federations in 1972.

> "European Kendo Championships will be held this year in Stockholm, 23rd and 24th September 1972. Those wishing to take part in the Individual championship or to go as visitors, please contact Count Robert von Sandor or myself. A first-class hotel costs 33 Sw.Kr. Per night."[3]

---

3 The To-Ken Society of Great Britain. *Programme 30*. September-October 1972, p 14.

ŌSHŪ KENDŌ RENMEI.

Official Register of Yūdansha – At 4th February, 1969.

No.	Name.		Dōjō.	Rank.	Date Promoted.
1.	R.A. Lidstone.		Nenriki.	Yondan	Oct. 1967.
2.	R.M. Knutsen.	Renshi.	Butokukan.	Yondan.	Oct. 1967.
3.	Hokage Kotaro.		Brussels.	Yondan.	1968.
4.	James Mathie.		Saineikan, Tokyo.	Sandan.	Oct. 1967.
5.	Gerd Wischnewski.		Wiesbaden.	Nidan.	1965.
6.	V.C. Cook.		Llangollen.	Nidan.	Aug. 1967.
7.	C. Chadwick.		Bushi-Budokai.	Nidan.	Aug. 1967.
8.	P. Kvalen.		Sussex. Univ.	Shōdan.	Jul. 1967.
9.	M. Tucker.		Nenriki.	Shōdan.	Aug. 1967.
10.	Robert von Sandor.		Swedish Kendo Ren.	Shōdan.	Jul. 1967.
11.	Jacques Dupont.		Brussels.	Shōdan.	Jul. 1967.
12.	B. Hilliard.		Nenriki.	Shōdan.	Aug. 1967.
13.	J. Self.		Sudbury.	Shōdan.	Mar. 1964.
14.	M. Grey.		Shintō-Ryū	Shōdan	Sept. 1964
15.	P. Armitage.		Sussex University	Shōdan	Nov. 1967.
16.	J. Nightingale.		Butokukan.	Shōdan	Nov. 1967.
17.	J. Clarke.		Zanshin.	Shōdan	Nov. 1967.
18.	R. Pollard.		Butokukan.	Shōdan	Nov. 1967.
19.	C. Stanton.		Sussex University	Shōdan	Nov. 1967.
20.	S. Gathorne Hardy		Malaysia Ken Ren	Shōdan	Nov. 1967.
21.	V. Harris		Nenriki.	Shōdan	Dec. 1967.
22.	P. Dawson.		Bujutsukai	Shōdan	Dec. 1967.
23.	B. Muter.		Bujutsukai	Shōdan	Dec. 1967.
24.	J. Hardy.		Butokukan	Shōdan	Dec. 1967.
25.	R. Kemp.		Bushi-Budokai	Shōdan	Jan. 1968.
26.	J. Piper.		Bushi-Budokai	Shōdan	Jan. 1968.
27.	J. Clarke.		Bushi-Budokai	Shōdan	Jan. 1968.
28.	W. Prytherch.		Coalville	Shōdan	Feb. 1968.
29.	A. Gomez.		France Ken Ren	Shōdan	Feb. 1968.
30.	R. Chartrain.		France Ken Ren	Shōdan	Feb. 1968.
31.	R. Calhoun.		France Ken Ren	Shōdan	Feb. 1968.
32.	C. Hamot.		France Ken Ren	Shōdan	Feb. 1968.
33.	Truong-Ngoc-An		France Ken Ren	Shōdan	Feb. 1968.

Could this be a contender for the first official European Kendo Championships? The event is confirmed in *L'Histoire du kendo en France* as members of a French Team selected from the FKR (la France Kendo Renmei) were excluded from participation.[4] Nevertheless, according to personal recollections from Jean-Claude Tuvi, the championship was eventually cancelled due mainly to a lack of response from the EKF member countries, which had fallen to only six at the time. We should also

---

4 L'Aminot, Tanguy, *L'Histoire du Kendo en France*. Accessed May 2016. http://chaken.fr/articlehistoire.html

ŌSHŪ KENDŌ RENMEI

Official Register of Yūdansha - At 4th February 1969.

No.	Name.	Dōjō.	Rank.	Date Promoted.
34.	B. Durand.	France Ken Ren	Shōdan	Feb.1968.
35.	V. Williams.	Nenriki	Shōdan	Mar.1968.
36.	R. Jarvis.	Nenriki	Shōdan	Mar.1968.
37.	R. Maddams.	Reading	Shōdan	Sept.1968.
38.	H. Hill.	Zanshin	Shōdan	Sept.1968.
39.	T.A.M. Pritchard.	Nenriki	Shōdan	Sept.1968.
40.	A.P. Hopson.	L.K.C.	Nidan	Sept.1964.
41.	Gaston Sterckx.	Belgian Ken Ren	Shōdan	Nov.1968.
42.	K.G. Feltham.	L.K.C.	Nidan	Sept.1964.
43.	G. Hodge.	Butokukan	Shōdan	Feb.1969.
44.	J. Richards.	Zanshin	Shōdan	Feb.1969.
45.	D. Baughurst.	Butokukan	Shōdan	Feb.1969.
46.	J. Jones.	Nenriki	Shōdan	Feb.1969.
47.	A. Smith.	L.K.C.	Shōdan	Feb.1969.
48.	D. Wolpe (Miss).	L.K.C.	Shōdan	Feb.1969.
49.	L. Bean.	Nenriki	Shōdan	Feb.1969.
50.	E. Schofield.	Nenriki	Shōdan	Feb.1969.
51.	J. Gibb.	Japan (Naginata)	Shōdan	Summer'68.

Left and above, Official Register of the Yudansha of the Ōshū Kendo Renmei. From records of the time (Author's collection)

bear in mind that the expense incurred for participation and to attend international competitions, team or individual, was down to the individual competitors, which would have been a prime consideration.[5]

In spite of these early events (or nearly events), it is now widely accepted that the 1st European Kendo Championship was held at Bletchley Leisure Centre in Milton Keynes on April 14, 1974.[6] I believe that this was agreed as a starting point for the newly renamed and now constituted European Kendo Federation. The numbering of subsequent EKCs start from this date. Nine European countries took part, with Great Britain captained by Victor Harris of Nenriki Dojo winning

---
5 Jean-Claude Tuvi (7-dan) is a respected senior member of French kendo CNK and was Vice President of the FKR.
6 The To-Ken Society of Great Britain. *Programme 32*. May-June 1974, p 5.

the team championships. The final with Belgium was a closely fought match with four draws and the final point going to Great Britain. The individual competition was won by Dave Todd of the Blyth Dojo.

The To-Ken report also confirmed that "Six Japanese experts had come especially for these championships representing the Imperial Palace, Police dojo, and the AJKF, and together with our good, friends Kikuchi (7-dan) from the Japanese Embassy in London and Fujii (5-dan), who acted as judges". According to the event program, the "six experts" were Kyōshi 8-dan Okuyama Kyōsuke, Kyōshi 7-dan Matsunaga Masami, Kyōshi 7-dan Hashimoto Akio, Kyōshi 7-dan Murayama Keisuke, Kyōshi 7-dan Kasahara Toshiaki, and Kyōshi 7-dan Satō Hironobu. The programme was signed by all of the sensei for its owner, Chris Buxton, who kindly allowed its reproduction here.

THE 1st EUROPEAN KENDO CHAMPIONSHIPS

with the co-operation of
JAPAN AIR LINES

Bletchley Leisure Centre Sunday, April 14th 1974

Front cover 1974 programme

Nine European countries—Austria, Belgium, France, Holland, Italy, Portugal, Sweden, Switzerland, and Great Britain—plus Australia and Japan were represented, and 47 competitors took part. The Opening Ceremony was performed by the Mayor of Milton Keynes, and those present included Sir Frank Bowden and Count Robert von Sandor. The opening address by Robert von Sandor, President of the European Kendo Federation, is reproduced on the second page of the programme.[7]

"Kendo was introduced to Europe about 10 years ago although there were small kendo-groups in Britain many years before. The European Kendo Federation now has nine member nations. The first European Championships is held in Britain as a tribute to the British contribution to the development of sword on this continent."

The results have also been handwritten inside. In the Team Competition 1st Place went to Great Britain, 2nd Place to Belgium, and 3rd to France. In the In-

---

[7] Official Programme of the 1st European Kendo Championships.

dividual Competition, the champion was David Todd (GB), 2nd Place was Jean-Claude Tuvi (France), and the two 3rd Places were taken by Jean-Pierre Niay (France) and Anders Markie (Sweden).

A letter was sent from AJKF to the BKA thanking them for their hospitality. It is also recorded in the history section of the British Kendo Association website that Great Britain took "all six gold medals" in these championships.[8] This probably refers to the five members of the team competition as well as the individual champion. Perhaps this was to generate some good publicity, as the event was well covered in the *Evening Standard*, *Daily Express*, and *Sunday Times* at the time.

The sensei in the 1974 programme

---

[8] Howell, John. *History of the British Kendo Association*. British Kendo Association. Accessed November 2015. http://www.britishkendoassociation.com/history-of-the-bka/

ON BEHALF of the British Kendo Association I would like to extend a very warm welcome to our fellow-kendoka who have come from seven other countries to join our own enthusiasts in the first European Kendo championships to be held in this country. Also a special welcome to members of the six-man mission of the International Kendo Federation who have come from Tokyo to help us as observers and judges.

This is an important occasion for our Association and we are grateful for the friendly enthusiasm and support we have received both from our own members and the Associations in other countries in arranging and taking part in these championships which will, I am sure, give further encouragement to Kendo in all the countries concerned. So, welcome to Britain and I hope enjoyable participation in the Championships.

Sir Frank Bowden, Bt.
President,
British Kendo Association.

KENDO — the art of the sword — is of Japanese origin. Although the technical performance of Kendo is typical Japanese, the deeper experience and mental effect is the same as the occidental swordsmanship of old times.

Masters of the sword, all over the world, proclaimed that swordsmanship is intended to improve the character of men and it is much more than simply "fencing".

The improvement is not only functional in the sense of producing a more efficient fighter-competitor but intrinsic in the sense of producing a better human being.

Therefore, traditionally, greater emphasis has been placed upon style, behaviour and character development in Kendo than on effectiveness with the sword as weapon.

However, Kendo is also competing and the "secret" of the art is the perfect balance between the discipline of integration as form, style, training in concentration and mental extension as well as the way in which a kendoman makes his "score".

Kendo was introduced to Europe about 10 years ago although there were small Kendo-groups in Britain many years before.

The European Kendo Federation now has nine member nations. The first European Kendo Championships is held in Britain as a tribute to the British contribution to the development of the art of the sword on this Continent.

Robert Sándor Count of Sándorfalva
President
European Kendo Federation

Address from Robert von Sandor

CONCLUSION

So ended the first 15 years of European kendo. A new chapter was beginning; one that would lead to perhaps a firmer establishment of kendo and a widening of horizons with more countries joining both the EKF and IKF. This probably came at a cost, however, with the loss of individuals caught up in the inevitable politics that are part and parcel of upheaval and development. In many ways the finding of the sets of armour in August 1957 by Roald Knutsen can be likened to the opening of Pandora's Box. Had they not been found, kendo would have made its way into our culture through a different route. Remembering that the last thing in Pandora's Box was "hope", we should all be grateful for the pioneering efforts of all of the early kendoka, as it was their struggles and sacrifices that paved the way for what we have now.

APPENDIX 1

Fujii Okimitsu

Fujii-sensei with Izawa Zensaku-Kyoshi, 8-dan and Roald Knutsen in 1968

I firmly believe that Fujii Okimitsu-sensei's contribution to kendo is hugely underrated and that he occupies the position as the "Forgotten Ronin" of British kendo, as he touched each and every part associated with kendo and iaido in the early days of the BKA. But it seems that he is deliberately ignored, not so dissimilar to the treatment in the final instance of Shiga Tadakatsu in France…' History ignored; history rewritten.

A graduate of Hosei University, he arrived in the UK in April 1967 after a discussion with Barry Morgan, the drummer of the 1960's band Blue Mink who Fujii-sensei would later manage in the UK. Morgan was also a session musician and had visited Japan on several occasions, for the first time in 1963. Fujii-sensei at that time was working in tour management and had arranged successful tours for the Oscar Petersen Trio, Count Basie and others including the Beatles on their first tour of Japan. Morgan and Fujii would become very good friends with Fujii-sensei staying at his house in London when he arrived in 1967.

His original intention had been to go to the West Coast of America after being offered a position there by the son of Duke Ellington, but Morgan convinced him that he should come to London instead. As his prime reason was to learn English conversation, Morgan stated quite categorically that Americans cannot speak English, so Fujii-sensei decided to go to England instead. However, Fujii-sensei had become very successful in his job and was only released after two years of training two replacements to take over his position.

For me as a complete and utter Beatles nut since they first exploded in the British swinging sixties, I always find it quite amazing to meet anyone involved with The Fab Four around that time. Therefore, Fujii-sensei's personal recollections were of course more than interesting to me. He simply stated that they were really OK guys with John being quite chatty. Later, during his time as manager of Blue Mink, he would again meet Paul McCartney who remembered him from their first visit to Japan. His other major recollection of the Beatles' first visit was the 16,000 lunchboxes that he ordered for the police and security staff who lined the route from Haneda airport to their hotel.

At university, he had spent six years studying law and psychology as it had been the wish of his family that he become a lawyer. During this time, he had learnt to play the saxophone but realised that he could never be good enough to be a professional. His thoughts then turned to music management as a profession and his law study would be put to good use on many occasions, as contracts had to be drawn up between the various performers and the government, who had the final say in who could and who could not tour in Japan.

Fujii-sensei started kendo at age six with Kamo Jisaku, a kendo and iaido Hanshi 8-dan from the Dai Nippon Butokukai, at a dojo named Kenseikai. This would be the name that Fujii-sensei would give his dojo in the UK following the visits of Kamo-sensei in 1973 and 1980.

Fujii-sensei continued his kendo during high school with Kyōshi 7-dan Itoyama Jukukichi, a former Navy officer, together with Kyōshi 7-dan Esaki Tamotsu. At high school he also trained at his local dojo under 10-dan Oasa Yuji, one of the special three referred to as 'the 10-dan of the Showa Era', together with Mochida Seiji and Saimura Gorō.

At Hosei University, the kendo teacher was Maruyama Yoshikazu, nicknamed the "Red Devil of Tokyo" as he would become red when he got angry and would focus on *tsuki* (thrust to the throat). Therefore, no-one would dare practise with him.

Fujii-sensei first met Roald Knutsen in the street at the Elephant and Castle when he had recognised that the latter was carrying kendo armour and introduced himself by asking about the armour. During the discussion, Knutsen became aware that Fujii-sensei was a 5-dan and he immediately insisted that he attend the sessions at the newly established Nenriki Dojo. According to Roald Knutsen:

> "I was walking down the Old Kent Road one evening on my way to the newly opened Nenriki Dojo in 1967 when I was hailed by Fujii-san, who had seen my kendo bōgu on my shoulder. He asked about kendo and came to the dojo. From then on we were friends and, of course, he proved very helpful right up to the time we lost touch in the late-1970s."

Fujii-sensei agreed, although somewhat reluctantly at first, to attend lessons and he quickly became the BKA's first resident Japanese sensei after Osaki Shintaro. He later established the Kenseikai Dojo group and the first long stay resident programme for UK kendo students in Japan based in Saga. It was instructed by Kamo Jisaku-sensei with the first students arriving in Saga in the same year. Kamo-sensei died in 1981, and the programme was then taken over by his successor, Sakai Yoshizo. Fujii-sensei was also responsible for bringing iaido sensei Haruna Matsuo to the U.K. in 1982.

Fujii-sensei took part in the 50th Anniversary of the Budokwai along with Knutsen-sensei. R. A. Lidstone was also present as a guest of honour. The event took place on Saturday November 30, 1968. Fujii-sensei and Knutsen-sensei demonstrated the Nihon Kendo Kata.

His personal history throws up some great stories, too many to list, but here at least is one of the best:

Fujii-sensei and the Salmon.
Whilst walking home one night after kendo practice with the late Terry Holt-sensei and Nenriki member Vaughn Williams (also now sadly no longer with us), perhaps just a little worse for wear after some liquid refreshment following the kendo session, there followed a heated discussion in which the BKA Chairman R.A. Lidstone was mentioned.

Fujii-sensei was carrying a fresh salmon that had been given to him that afternoon for a restaurant that he was running. It was a very large piece of fish. The conversation then became extremely disrespectful and insulting towards Lidstone. In a flash as a direct response, Fujii-sensei very promptly laid the culprit Vaughn Williams flat out on the floor by whacking him with the salmon. It's hard to imagine this course of action by today's standards, but Fujii-sensei held Lidstone in such a very high regard and respected his contribution to kendo spanning nearly 40 years. So it was just not acceptable for a student to speak badly of such a man 'drunk or otherwise'.

Fujii-sensei also had a good relationship with the Otani family and one day was summoned to the household. Tomio's father Masutaro instructed Fujii-sensei that he must take in hand his son's kendo teaching as it lacked in any real fundamentals.

This relationship did create some difficulties as the understanding seems to have been construed by Roald Knutsen and others that Fujii-sensei was being headhunted to the British Kendo Council, which was under the control of Abe Kenshiro-sensei.

The organisation and Otani were seen as a direct threat and challenge to the newly formed BKA. According to correspondence between Lidstone and Knutsen, other BKA members were also liaising and quite openly practising at his Acton dojo, possibly quite unaware of the issues and problems that were being perceived together with the quite intense discussions that were taking place to try and resolve matters.

In a communication to R.A. Lidstone from Roald Knutsen early in 1968 he states that:

> "On Friday evening, I think we should have a word with the Nenriki Committee about the London Kendo Club and Otani Tomio. It would be desirable that matters should be clearly fully understood by the members there and I have explained something of it to Mr Fujii. I am sure that Otani would dearly love to have Fujii at his dojo to capitalise on the said visitor's prestige for his people. It would certainly be against our policy though I have no objection to them visiting us (provided there is no trouble or hint of partnership)."

Otani Tomio was then something of a nemesis to Roald Knutsen, adding further to the driving force behind the motivation to solidly develop kendo and iaido not only here in the UK but also throughout Europe, and to have it run by reputable organisations.

Many years have now passed since those frontier days and any differences that existed have since been reconciled. Fujii-sensei lived in Cornwall where he practised and taught kendo and iaido up until he passed away in April 2017.

APPENDIX 2

Roald Knutsen

Roald Knutsen with Jim Mathie, Saineikan dojo, Tokyo, October 3, 1967

Roald Knutsen[1] was born in Hertfordshire in 1933 of Anglo-Norwegian parents and educated at The Perse School, Cambridge, and Watford Grammar School. After studying art and design he served as a regular in the Intelligence Corps.

This was followed by a successful career in graphic design, choreographing complex medieval combat sequences for a computer film project in England and the USA, studying arms and armour at the Royal Armouries, and writing.

For the past half-century, he has practised traditional Japanese sword related arts under a succession of famous Japanese masters and was awarded a senior master's licence, the instructor status of Renshi, and a commemorative *menjō* certificate marking the Meiji Centenary in 1968.

He has researched and written extensively about the Japanese warrior traditions and aspects of Japanese history. As a highly-accomplished artist he has produced many fine works of art over the years.

Without his determination, British kendo might not have emerged and become what it is today; the three kendo armours might also still be sitting undisturbed in the cupboard at the London Judo Society.

In relation to the above I had asked Knutsen-sensei specifically about the grades and awards as I was curious about what kind of system had existed in those early years. His 3-dan was given to him by Hanshi 8-dan Nakamura Kishiro in London when he visited in the mid-1960s. This sensei came to London and they spent quite some time together at the Tavistock Hotel in Bloomsbury and at the dojo in Kennington. He was the Ibaraki prefecture Representative in the Upper House of the Diet. He considered that in order to give kendo a firm footing in the UK, Knutsen-sensei must have a rank and accordingly gave him 3-dan. The ZNKR later awarded him Renshi status. His 3-dan *menjo* was written out on Tavistock Hotel notepaper and his Renshi *menjo* still hangs on his wall at home.

His 4-dan advancement came on the considered advice of Hanshi Ozawa-sensei and Kyōshi Arai-sensei, and other high level sensei. After that, all grade promotions were made by the BKA and EKR after direct consultation with these senior Japanese advisors and others of the ZNKR.

The commemorative *menjō* he received in 1968, was a special distinction for "his efforts in kendo (and Japan) on the occasion of the celebrations marking the

---
1 Budden, Paul. "Three Ages of British Kendo". In *Biographical Portraits* Volume IX, ed. Cortazzi, Hugh. Folkestone, Kent: Renaissance Books, 2015. 48.

100th Anniversary of the Restoration of the Emperor Meiji"; he was one of less than twenty non-Japanese so honoured.

Books by Roald Knutsen:

Japanese Polearms, Published by Holland Press (1963)

Rediscovering Budo, Published by Global Oriental (2004)

Japanese Spears, co-authored with his wife Patricia Knutsen, Published by Global Oriental (2004)

Sun Tzu and the Art of Medieval Japanese Warfare, Published by Global Oriental Ltd (2006)

Tales of Enshin, the Reluctant Samurai, Published by Renaissance Books, an Imprint of Global Books, (2010) *Tengu,* Published by Global Oriental Ltd (2011)

References and Principal Sources

Roald Knutsen - personal letters, records and recollections
Jacques Dupont
Nagao Susumu - research and advice
Kurata Yoshihiro - *1885 Japan in London*
Takizawa Kenji - recollections of his Father
Judo Magazines - author's personal collection
Prabook.org
The To-ken Society, London
John Bowen and the London Budokwai
Wikipedia
IMDb
Tanguy L'Aminot - *L' Histoire du kendo en France*
Alain Floquet - Fondateur de l'Aikibudo 9-dan Hanshi
Jean-Claude Tuvi
Jean-Marc Papadacci - Professeur 4-dan Président du CERA (Centre International de l'Aikibudo)

Photos:

Jacques Dupont
Judo Magazines from the author's personal collection
Roald Knutsen
George McCall
Nevil Shute Foundation
Chris Buxton
The British Library 'Posters of the Japanese Village'
Ohsaki Shintaro
The family of the late Yasuzo Ishigaki-sensei
Kazuhiro Murase-sensei, President of Shimazu Shobo Publishing
Jean-Claude Tuvi
Alain Floquet

About the Author

Paul Budden was born in 1949 in Cheltenham England. When not involved with kendo he continues to assist in running an established international exhibition company. Having graduated in kendo to Kyoshi 7-dan, his involvement has increased over some 30 odd years both as the founder and Kancho of Kodokan Kendo UK (since 1980), where both adults and junior practitioners attend regular practice sessions, and also as Technical Director for the Maltese Kendo Federation. As an international coach he now divides his time between the U.K., Malta and throughout Europe (including Eastern Europe), running courses, assisting with seminars including charity events and international competitions. He is also the author of *Looking at a Far Mountain: A Study of Kendo Kata*; *Devil's Gloves and the One Cut – An introduction to Ono-ha Itto Ryu Kata*; *Three Ages of British Kendo* written for the Japan Society, London in *Biographical Portraits volume IX* and *A Truly British Samurai: The Exceptional Charles Boxer (1904-2000)*. He was a member of the British team that won bronze in 1987 at the European Kendo Championships in Malmo and has visited Japan on numerous occasions for study and practice in a continuing quest for knowledge and improvement—'The ultimate is unattainable but the journey is educational and enjoyable.' He is also the Official Speaker at the European Kendo Championships for the European Kendo Federation and was Co-Organising Director of the 12th World Kendo Championships in Glasgow, 2003, for the British Kendo Association.

Paul believes very strongly in maintaining the traditional interpretation of kendo and is dedicated to the classical practice of koryu and the philosophy that kendo personifies.

Copyright © 2017 Paul Budden. All Rights Reserved.

www.ingramcontent.com/pod-product-compliance
Lightning Source LLC
Chambersburg PA
CBHW041533220426
43662CB00002B/46